CLOSING
TECHNIQUES
(That Really Work!)

THIRD EDITION

Stephan Schiffman

Adams Media
Avon, Massachusetts

To AFS, *again*

Published by
Adams Media, an F+W Publications Company
57 Littlefield Street, Avon, MA 02322. U.S.A.
www.adamsmedia.com

ISBN: 1-58062-857-5

Printed in the United States of America.

J I H G F E D C B

Library of Congress Cataloging-in-Publication Data
Schiffman, Stephan.
Closing techniques / Stephan Schiffman. — 3rd ed.
p.   cm.
Includes index.
ISBN 1-58062-857-5
1. Selling. I. Title.
HF5438.25.S334 2004
658.85—dc22
2003020361

This book is available at quantity discounts for bulk purchases.
For information, call 1-800-872-5627.

Contents

Part Three: Rethinking Your Relationship with the Prospect / 55

Acknowledgments

The following people helped make this book a reality: Brandon Toropov, Lynne Einleger, Steve Bookbinder, Michele Reisner and, especially, Daniele, Jennifer, and Anne, whose patience and understanding were invaluable. I'd also like to acknowledge here all the families of salespeople, who put up with the deadlines, quotas, difficult prospects, hard sales, and obsessive work that are part of any good salesperson's life.

Introduction

Is closing really the most difficult part of the sale?

You'd think so to hear people talk. Most salespeople are terrified by the idea of closing. Often, they view it as a final conflict with their prospects, the point at which they must pull out the heavy artillery and finally get the job done.

But even though closing the sale is the part of the job nearly every salesperson dreads, it can actually be the easiest part of the sales cycle. That's the argument I make in this book, and I firmly believe that if you follow the steps you're about to see outlined, you'll agree with me about the ease of closing by the time you finish this program and implement it. You won't agree with me because you appreciate the ideas on some abstract level. You'll agree with me because your commission checks will be bigger, you'll find that you're working more efficiently than ever, and you aren't scared of your prospects any more.

I've worked with small companies, medium-sized companies, and *Fortune* 500 companies. I've trained over 350,000 salespeople in over 900 companies, throughout the world. The ideas on the pages of this book have worked for them, and they can work for you.

I'm going to show you how to integrate the closing process into a productive, professional sales cycle. I'm going to show you how to turn prospects into allies, not adversaries. I'm going to show you how to make manipulative tricks and high-pressure techniques obsolete.

Read what follows. Give it an honest try. And you will change your career for the better.

Stephan Schiffman
New York, New York

Part One

The Fundamentals

CHAPTER 1

A Third of a Season

I believe that selling is not complex.

Surprising as it may seem, that's a minority opinion. There are a lot of sales experts out there who will tell you that I'm dead wrong, and that sales is a very complicated matter involving elaborate levels of persuasion and interpersonal manipulation. These people have written a lot of books. Most of the modern sales books, I think, are really rehashes of old, essentially confrontational techniques that came into vogue in the 1950s—or even earlier.

I Decided to Read a Lot of Books

As part of the research for this project, I bought and read every single book having to do with the topic "closing the sale" that I could get my hands on. After reading them all, I found out that most of them had essentially the same message. If anything, the emphasis would vary slightly from book to book, but the central idea was identical.

Each book stressed either outside research or in-person "probing"—and then making a presentation meant to close the sale. And each of these books—there were dozens of them—ended up giving you specific techniques that you could employ to *convince the person to buy.*

And my feeling, after reviewing those books, was that this common (actually, nearly universal) approach to training salespeople was one of the chief reasons people often feel that sales as a career is ridiculous today.

Closing the Sale—The "Tricks of the Trade"

Closing the sale is not a gimmick, but you'd never know it from reading the books that are out there. One of the books I came across passed on 187 different tricks to use with prospects, each designed to convince him or her to buy. There are a lot of them. Most are remarkably dumb.

One trick they tell you to pull is to roll your uncapped fountain pen across the desk to the prospect, who will pick it up to avoid being spattered. You then quickly slip your order form underneath the pen and say something like, "Well, since you've already got the pen in your hand and the contract in front of you, you might as well sign." (I am not kidding. Someone really wrote this stuff.)

Another trick is to draw a vertical line down a piece of paper, asking the prospect to work with you to develop "pros" and "cons," then making the prospect promise you that, if, "working together," you and the prospect come up with more good elements than liabilities, the prospect loses the game and has to buy. (Of course, if the prospect can come up with enough negatives to outnumber your positives, then *you* lose the game and have to leave the prospect's office.)

By the way, someone actually tried that two-column technique with Mike, one of the salespeople in our office. You want to hear how it went? The salesperson, who did not ask Mike *anything* about how he planned to use the product he had to offer, said, "All right, Mike, here's what we're going to do. I'm going to draw a line down the middle of this sheet. Here's one column that says reasons to buy, and another that says reasons not to buy."

The salesperson then proceeded to list about twenty "reasons" for Mike to buy what he had to offer. Then he looked at Mike and said, "Okay, your turn. Why don't you want to buy this?"

Mike said, "Because I need to think about it."

The salesperson wrote that down and said, "Okay, need to think about it. What's the next reason?"

Mike said, "Because I need to think about it."

The salesperson said, "Okay, looks like we're all done. Now look at this sheet. On my side, I have twenty reasons for you to go with us. On your side, you have two. Can you give me even one more reason why you shouldn't buy from us?"

Mike said, "Yes. I don't like you."

That, not surprisingly, was the end of the conversation and the end of that sales cycle.

There are dozens of other ridiculous techniques the "experts" want you to use.

Here's my favorite. You're supposed to look at the prospect with big, hungry, puppy-dog eyes and say, "Mr. Prospect, if you don't buy from me, I'll lose my job." That's right—you're actually supposed to try to shame the prospect into concluding that if you don't get the sale, you're going to lose your house, wander the streets, and perhaps yield your first-born child to the boss.

Now, let me tell you something. If you're willing to say that, I'm going to go out on a limb here and suggest that you are looking at your career in the wrong way. If you're willing to place your relationship with the prospect on the hope that pity, rather than trust in your ability to deliver the goods, will carry the day, then you should probably think about getting out of sales. If you believe anyone who tells you that the way to initiate a business relationship is to encourage the prospect to think, not of his or her goals, but of your problems, then I respectfully submit that you should be looking for another line of work.

But if, like me, you feel a natural revulsion at the idea of saying that to a prospect; if you feel there must be some way to build a bridge that allows you to deal with the prospect as a fellow business person, rather than as a supplicant, or someone to be manipulated, or an opponent; if you prefer dealing in solutions to pleading poverty or playing games—then keep reading. I wrote this book for you.

The Dangers of "It Works for Me"

Some people may claim to use the methods I just outlined— and their innumerable variants—with success. Don't listen to them.

Point One: Unless you are completely incompetent, you will close about one-third of all your sales whether or not you use stupid techniques like the ones I've just mentioned. Let me put this idea into a sports context. The worst baseball team of the twentieth century was probably the 1962 New York Mets, a legendary squad of "has-beens and never-weres" that has been the subject of more books, articles, jokes, and stories than most pennant-winning clubs. Now, the New York Mets lost more games that year than any other modern club. But you know what? They also *won* forty games.

They won forty games! Isn't that remarkable? Suppose the team captain sits down with a reporter after an old-timer's game and says, "Well, you've got to remember, we didn't lose 'em all. So I guess having the lowest fielding percentage in the league was a plus. I guess posting the lowest team batting average in the National League must have been good for some-thing. I guess having two twenty-game losers and another guy who won three and lost seventeen really was a pretty good starting rotation. I guess having a reliever whose earned-run average was 4.53, who never saved a single game, and who walked a whole lot more batters than he struck out was a real stroke of genius on our part. So what if he was out of the big leagues the next year. We won forty games!"

What do you think of that assessment?

More to the point, which team would you rather play for? The 1962 Mets, who stank up the joint but had forty wins, or the 1962 Yankees, the team that followed through on a decades-long commitment to excellence and professionalism—and, at the end of the year, after having appeared in their twenty-third World Series in thirty-six years, won the championship?

Point Two: You are also going to lose about one-third of your sales no matter what you do. Here again, we can look to the baseball diamond. Those 1962 Yankees lost fifty-three games out of 162, almost exactly a third of a season. Their competition showed up. Some days the Yankees lost. It was part of the game. And it's part of your game as a salesperson, too. You're going to get one-third and you're going to lose one-third. Pretty much everyone in your league can count on that.

Point Three: What counts is what you make happen with the remaining third. Not the one-third you're going to win anyway. Not the one-third you're going to lose anyway. The last-place team in the American League in 1962 was forty-seven and a half games behind the Yankees; the Mets were sixty games behind the first-place team in their league. Take the average of the two, and you're looking at about fifty-four games—one-third of the season. That's the difference between the pennant-winner and the team in the cellar. The one-third of the games that could go either way. Those are the ones you have to try to win.

Don't Use the Cheap Stuff

It is the premise of this book that you can't win those "middle-third" sales by using the amateur techniques of tricking, manipulating, or lying to your prospects and customers. If you don't believe it, you are certainly welcome to try the kinds of maneuvers I've been complaining about in this chapter. But I should tell you here, I've trained hundreds of thousands of salespeople, in 900 companies throughout the world, and I've seen the kinds of people who win those "middle-third" sales. Trust me. They don't play like the Mets did in 1962. They play with pride, like the 1962 Yankees. They make commitments and keep them. They are pros.

CHAPTER 2

The Definition of Sales

Closing is certainly part of selling—but what is selling?

You can get a lot of different answers from a lot of different people. Any number of experts might define sales in terms of making someone else do something that you want them to do. Or projecting yourself so strongly ("standing out from the other messages") that an organization basically has no choice but to stop ignoring you. Or delivering a competitive advantage to someone in your target organization. Or knowing an industry inside and out so that you hear about opportunities first and act quickly. Or finding a need and filling it. (This one is particularly dangerous in my opinion, because it doesn't take into account the fact that, these days, when someone needs a copier, or an insurance policy, or a window-washer, or whatever, that person is not likely to sit around "needing" it for long, but is instead going to pick up the phone and call someone and have the problem resolved by four that afternoon!)

Simplify, Simplify

My definition of sales is a simple one.

For me, sales is *asking people what they do, how they do it, when they do it, where they do it, why they do it, and who they do it with—and then helping them do it better.*

It's from this perspective—and not from any other—that we will be approaching the task of closing sales.

For too many salespeople today, closing is a little like the kids' game, Pin the Tail on the Donkey. You walk into a room, are blindfolded and spun around, and are pointed in the general direction of your goal. Maybe you hit what you're supposed to every once in a while, but usually you don't.

It was great fun, but you don't need to bother with it now. You're not a kid anymore, and there's no reason for you to play games with your career. If you follow the ideas I outline in this book, you'll enter the closing stage with your prospect with your eyes wide open. And that's the way it should be.

CHAPTER 3

No Gimmicks

Rather than stringing you along for the rest of the book, I'm going to pass along, right here and right now, the key technique you'll use and adapt to close your sales. I want you to know before we go any further how simple I believe good selling is—or, at any rate, can be. This is the technique that I use myself, and that I teach in my seminars. It's not a gimmick. It's a nonconfrontational, straightforward approach that is rooted in the relationship I've developed with a prospect.

The Conclusion of the Process

When I've made the *right presentation* to my prospect, which requires *getting the right information*, which I've assembled after *prospecting correctly*, I simply say this:

Mr. Prospect, it makes sense to me. What do you think?

No gimmicks. No tricks. No mind games.

Now, only two things can happen once I've said that. The prospect can either say, "Yes, it makes sense to me, too," in which case we'll begin to work together. Or the prospect can say, "No, it doesn't make sense to me," in which case I say, "Oh—why not?" And I begin to refine the presentation so I can, after isolating whatever problems the prospect has, continue to move the sales cycle forward.

Closing is a logical progression of the sales cycle, nothing more and nothing less.

The Keys to Building a Business Relationship

Closing is agreeing. Closing is the simplest, most straightforward part of the whole cycle. It's not something to get worked up about. It's what should—what must—happen next if you have done your work in the preceding stages of the sale, which we'll be discussing in detail a little later in the book.

If you've done the early work properly, your approach should be simply to come to a point of *mutual* agreement with the prospect about why it makes sense for you to work together. You will, I think, be surprised at how much tension and stress will disappear from your life once you approach your job in this way.

In this book you will learn to *gain agreement* directly and confidently, without being overbearing, for the business. You will learn not to rely on gimmicks. You will learn how to work with your prospect as one professional works with another.

There are any number of variations on and adaptations of the simple approach I've outlined in this brief chapter. We'll be looking at all those in the pages that follow. Right now, however, I want you to bear in mind the principle on which this entire book is based, namely that *closing a sale is a natural outgrowth of your earlier work, not a separate conclusion you somehow impose upon your prospect.*

Closing is simple; when executed properly, it's the least intimidating aspect of the sales cycle. It's only when we try to make it complicated that it gets scary.

CHAPTER 4

Objections That Aren't

The "objection" that every other book teaches you to "turn around" may be nothing more than a question.

You may be used to treating these exchanges with your prospects as challenges to your own competence or to the quality of your product. If that's the case, you'll need to change the way you react to your prospect.

Block That Snappy Comeback!

Not long ago, I made what I considered to be a very solid presentation to a major advertising agency in New York City. At the end of it, my prospect delivered a long list of problems he said he had with our company: how other people in the industry had dealt with other kinds of firms, how our client list didn't meet his expectations, how the kind of selling we were good at dealing with was different than the kind he asked his people to engage in, and on and on. I was sitting there, fighting my instinct to turn around each of his responses. Before I could even say anything though, he said, "But I'll tell you something, Steve. I like the way you look at the salesperson as a professional problem-solver, like a consultant. So we're going to go with you."

I've never been so glad not to get a word in edgewise in my life.

Can you imagine what would have happened if I'd followed my natural instinct to check each of his objections and "turn them around"?

It's natural to want to rebut what appears to be an accusation or a denigration. But it's not the way to build a partnership.

I think the first job of any modern salesperson is not, as so many would have you believe, to persuade, but rather to *listen*. We have to *listen* to each and every objection, for the simple reason that, often, it's not an objection at all, but a statement or a question. Sometimes, as in the case above, we must also be careful not to manufacture objections where there are none.

How many times have you overreacted in such a situation? How many sales have you lost that fell into that "middle third" category because you *turned a concern into an objection* for a client?

Our objective is not to polarize the situation. Our objective is to *help the prospect do his or her job*. That's what wins "middle third" sales—knowing what the prospect does, listening to the prospect's concerns, and helping the prospect do his or her job better. Period.

No Contests

You're going to be reading a lot more about responses from prospects and customers, but for right now I want you to remember that your first step in dealing with a perceived objection should be to *check your natural instinct to turn it around*—and, instead, simply listen. You're not in a contest with your prospect. You're not playing a game in which you "win" if you close the sale and your prospect "wins" if you don't. The minute you move into that realm of confrontational sales, you've polarized the exchange. I'm not saying that there are no salespeople who make a living this way. I am saying that salespeople who close their "middle third" don't get hung up in ping-pong matches with their prospects.

Think you hear an objection? Listen first. Is what you're hearing really a disguised question or statement? If so, how would you respond if it were phrased as such?

CHAPTER 5

A Brief Review of the Sales Cycle

Because this book is about closing, we'll be spending a great deal of time talking about the final stage of the sales cycle. But as we've seen, that stage is really only an outgrowth of three earlier stages, stages that cannot be omitted if you expect to win those "middle third" sales.

Here you will find a thumbnail sketch of the main elements of the sales cycle. For a more detailed look at the cycle, you may want to pick up a copy of my book *Power Sales Presentations*, which covers the topic in depth.

Stage One: Prospecting

Also called "qualifying," prospecting is when you and the person you're talking to determine that you're mutually interested in discussing whether or not there might be an application for your proposed solution. That doesn't mean that you're certain the individual you're dealing with wants to buy your product or service. You're simply making sure that the person is willing to talk about the potential usefulness of what you have to offer.

In short, you're overseeing the contact's transition from

"suspect" (someone who may or may not be able to use the product or service) to "prospect" (someone whom you've determined is interested to learn more about what you have to offer).

For many salespeople, the prospecting stage takes the form of cold calls.

Stage Two: Interviewing

This is where you get detailed information about the goals of your prospect in order to determine what you'll say later on, during your presentation. It often takes the form of your first in-person interview.

Typically, there are three basic questions to ask at this stage. They have to do with the past ("Mr. Smith, have you ever worked with XYZ Widgets before?"), the present ("Mr. Smith, what are you presently using when it comes to widgets?"), and the future ("Mr. Smith, what are your future plans in the widget area?"). All three questions can be expanded with "how" and "why" variations.

Stage two often concludes with your *brief* description of your product or service and the prospect's affirmation, a "That sounds interesting" remark or something similar to it. In many cases, you schedule a second meeting with the prospect; in any event, you will want to confirm or verify your information.

Stage Three: Presentation

This is where you supply more specific data about the benefits of the product or service *as those benefits directly relate to that particular prospect.*

Of course, there are a lot of things you can point out to the prospect at this point, but they tend to break down to three categories: *features, benefits,* and *proof.* A feature of your widget might be that it's easy to clean. A benefit might be that it increases the department's production (and not, that it has, say, a high input-output rate—that would be another feature). Proof of your widget's usefulness might be the fact that it was singled out for an industry honor by a trade magazine.

Many salespeople get sidetracked into discussing features and proof with their prospects. These are important elements, but they should support the main thrust of your presentation, the benefits your prospect is likely to enjoy as a result of working with you.

During your presentation, focus on the benefit first. Focus on the ways in which you can help your prospect do his or her job better. Wherever possible, use *verbatim* the suggestions and comments you received in stage two.

Stage Four: Closing

If the proper groundwork has been laid, and if there is in fact a good potential match between what you have to offer and what your prospect would like to be doing, closing the sale is quite simple. You make the assumption that you can help your prospect and you ask for the sale in terms the prospect will find unthreatening. You try to get things started.

Will you get shot down? Sometimes. But what's the alternative? Continuing to prattle on about how wonderful your widgets are? The prospect has heard that already!

Closing means confidently asking for the sale without polarizing the relationship.

Moving Ahead

The sales cycle we've just outlined is a dynamic paradigm. That's a fancy way of saying that you can't sit still. If you're in the prospecting stage, your objective is to move the cycle along to the interviewing stage. If you're in the interviewing stage, your objective is to move the cycle along to the presentation stage. If you're in the presentation stage, your objective is to get to a point where you can confidently ask for the business, because you feel strongly that you've identified a way for your prospect to do his or her job better.

CHAPTER 6

Why People Buy

There are basically two reasons why people decide to buy from a salesperson.

They either *act to accomplish something that they themselves perceived as important before the salesperson showed up* or *act in response to an opportunity the salesperson brings to their attention.*

The First Category of Sale

The first kind of sale is one you should be able to close the vast majority of the time. In fact, it's actually quite similar to order taking. There may be some price resistance or some similar obstacle, but in most cases this first kind of buy decision is one that's relatively easy for you to elicit. After all, the prospect knows about the existing problem already. You show up; you demonstrate how you can solve the problem.

That first kind of sale falls into the "third-you're-going-to-win" category.

The Second Category of Sale

The other kind of sale, however, takes some more work on your part. This is where your communication skills and, perhaps even more important, *listening* skills come into play. You must *learn* what your prospect has to do, and make an intelligent proposal that will show your prospect how to do the job better.

That second kind of sale falls into that "third-you-need-to-win-to-play-at-the-top-level" category.

The second kind of sale takes skill and practice. You're likely to bobble it a couple of times, then get better at it, and, with a good, solid, big-league effort, master it.

But it won't happen overnight. And it certainly won't happen if you don't master the art of *listening* to your prospect.

Opportunism

There's more to it than that, though; a certain flexibility, the ability to see—or, perhaps more accurately, intuit—where you can offer a realistic solution, even a solution that has not been considered before. Closing the second kind of sale requires, in short, that you think on your feet and become something of an opportunist.

When I say you must become an opportunist, I don't use the word in the sense you may be thinking of. Often, these days, when we hear that word we think of someone who is crafty, cunning, conniving, and ruthlessly ambitious. This is not the kind of opportunism I have in mind!

No, the opportunism I'm suggesting you develop is rooted simply in the idea that you *keep an eye open for opportunities* that will benefit both you and your prospect. My kind of opportunism has to do with calling someone up, finding out important facts about that person's organization, explaining what our own product or service does, and then making a commitment to help that organization use what we have to offer to do the job better. That's opportunism that lifts up, rather than draws down.

The seller who forgets that he or she is an initiator, an opportunist, is the one who is simply waiting to run into sales. That means basing your career on those first-category sales. Don't do it. You shouldn't *reject* first-category sales, of course, but you shouldn't think that you've done your job as well as you can do it if you don't reach beyond them, either.

Avoid Complacency

A great many salespeople get lulled into believing that they are touching all the bases when they're really not. They get seduced by repeat customers and the like. They don't initiate. They become order-takers. They limp along and meet minimum goals. And you know what? They pay a price for that complacency.

For one thing, their incomes tend to fluctuate quite a bit. That's not good sales form, at least not in my book. A solid professional salesperson should, in my opinion, be able to hit and maintain a target income level over an extended period of time. My own definition of a *successful* salesperson is someone who can hit an aggressive income target—say, between $75,000 and $125,000 per year—and maintain that income level for a period of ten years.

For another thing, complacent salespeople are *extremely vulnerable.* If a new competitor enters the market, or there's a downturn in the economy, or there's some other unforeseen development that cuts into their customer base, they suddenly find themselves with nothing in the pipeline. What's even scarier, they find themselves rusty—at best—when it comes to taking charge of their careers, as they inevitably must.

Don't get complacent. Take charge. Take responsibility for initiating contact and increasing your business base, and stay flexible enough to open up new avenues of opportunity with your product or service. Top salespeople focus on getting new, untapped business *and* servicing prospects who already seem able to use what they have to offer. Be one of those top salespeople.

(By the way, if you do this, you'll be issuing yourself an important insurance policy of sorts. More than one company has reacted to market pressures or economic shifts by laying off those salespeople who could not prove themselves capable of *developing new business*. My guess is that before too long, the days when a salesperson could ride along on "fell-in-my-lap" sales and low-maintenance repeat business will be over in just about every major industry.)

Openings
Precede Closings

This is a book about closing sales, so I don't want to spend too
much time on the issue of prospecting. But it is a topic of
tremendous importance to your sales success, so I want to talk
about it briefly here.

Some sales writers suggest that you spend enormous
amounts of time researching the target company before you
make your first call. Any number of sales reps will tell you stories about how they mailed a brick to a prospect to get attention, or sent a photograph of themselves, or faxed along a
mysterious note, or even sent flowers.

Sometimes these techniques win you a moment of
someone's time on the phone. Sometimes they don't. The real
question, though, is whether or not they're particularly effective
in getting you *appointments,* and I have my doubts on that score.

Initial Contacts

My suggestion on the subject of making initial contacts with
potential customers is that you standardize your approach,
learn about your own resulting numbers, make a plan, and then
stick to it. All too often, gimmicks like the ones outlined above
are employed when salespeople have fallen into a polarized way

of looking at their contacts with potential customers. "So they're not returning my calls over at ABC Company, eh? Well, I'll show them. I'm going to get that account (or, that appointment) if it's the last thing I do."

Rather than spend all day composing the perfect note to accompany those dozen roses you were planning to send, why not take a look at your long-range prospecting plan? Rather than focus on research in the library that's months, years, or even decades old, why not use an information-gathering technique that gives you facts that are accurate as of *right now?* Why not fine-tune your cold calling script? Why not figure out how many dials (numbers you call) it takes to yield a completed call (a contact with a real, live decision maker)? Why not figure out how many completed calls result in an in-person visit? Why not figure out how many in-person visits you typically have to go on to get a single sale? Why not track these elements of your sales work for a month, see how the numbers come out, and get honest-to-goodness hard data on what it takes for you to keep sales coming through the pipeline?

(By the way, the ratios you shoot for could look something like this: twenty completed calls to five visits to one sale. The ratio of dials to completed calls will vary widely from industry to industry.)

At the end of this book, you'll find specific examples that will help you develop your own effective cold calling scripts. The topic of prospecting by phone is covered in much greater detail in my book *Cold Calling Techniques (That Really Work!).* I do want to say here, though, that my experience has been that the single most reliable way to increase sales is to fine-tune your prospecting work.

So ask yourself: Rather than focusing exclusively on what you do at the end of the cycle, could you be prospecting more effectively at the *beginning* of the cycle—and improving your performance with comparative ease?

Part Two

Breakthrough Ideas for Closing Success

CHAPTER 8

A Few Words about the Ideas You'll Find in this Section of the Book

In this part of the book, I'm going to pass along some general observations and techniques that will probably be helpful to you in your everyday sales work and, without altering your existing pattern too much, help you increase your closing rate. In other words, you will find here a number of helpful "stand-alone" ideas that will require little change in the way you approach your everyday sales work.

In the third section of *Closing Techniques (That Really Work!)*, we'll take a more in-depth look at your contacts with your prospect, and we'll begin to implement some of the long-term changes you will need to make in order to make the final move toward those "middle-third" sales.

When you try to make one of the ideas in this section work for you, give it a while to take root. Don't follow an idea for a day or two, then assume that you've derived the full benefit from it. It's been said that a habit, good or bad, takes twenty-one days to develop. Think how long our bad sales habits have had to take hold! Try to incorporate each of the ideas that follow in this second section for a three-week period—and give the good habits a chance to become permanent, too.

CHAPTER 9

Know Your Product or Service—and Be Creative in Considering What It Can Do for Someone

Part of the secret of getting those all-important "middle-third" sales is being obsessive about all the possible applications your product or service may have. Most salespeople don't concentrate enough on this issue. They assume that the people in production or someone else on the front line will "take care of all that." Maybe those people have a job to do, but so do you! You must *know* what you sell.

Closing is the act of formally beginning your new relationship with someone whose job you can make easier. You can't expect to begin a relationship like that in earnest unless you know exactly *how* you will be helping!

A Story

I worked recently with a huge regional bank. Management was disappointed with the performance of some of its salespeople, and my job was to find out what the problem was. It turned out that the salespeople in question had been trained on all the various features of the (extremely complex) financial products they were selling—but not on how consumers would actually *use* those products! In other words, they had all the technical knowledge they needed, and then some, but they still lacked the practical knowledge of how things worked in the minds of the people who would ultimately be likely to buy. Put more directly, they weren't thinking like consumers.

Memorizing the manuals and the spec sheets and the brochures is not enough. Have you actually *used* your product or service as a prospect might? If you haven't, do so! If you have, don't stop there! You must know absolutely everything there is to know about what you have to offer. You must know it inside and out, and you must be ready to outline for prospects exactly how they can make their lives easier by implementing your solutions. In fact, you have to be able to highlight *new* uses for your product or service that your prospect and even your superiors have not yet considered!

Stop and think about what you sell. How can you adapt your existing product or service to satisfy a prospect?

In my books and seminars, I discuss the idea of product/ service "malleability"; the word means "flexibility" or "capacity of being adapted." I want to take this opportunity to review some of those ideas here, because they're extremely important for the salesperson whose objective is to close the "middle-third" sales.

Something is malleable if it can take another shape. Dentists use gold and silver for fillings because of the malleability of those metals; they are easily manipulated and provide a complete, secure fit over and within a cavity. Along the same lines, you might want to think about the ways your product or service can be adjusted or customized for new prospects to meet specific requirements.

Now let's take a look at a simple example. Suppose you're

in the paper clip business. How many ways do you think you could use paper clips? Obviously, you can think of a paper clip as a small metal item used to fasten sheets of paper together. But if you stop and think about it for a moment, you'll realize that people use paper clips for all kinds of different purposes. Some people twist them into makeshift cotter pins; some people use them to clean out hard-to-reach places on office equipment; some people use them to fix eyeglasses; some people make decorative chains out of them. I personally have used (with great care!) two paper clips as a tiny clamp to extract a stubborn disk that would not eject from my computer's drive. (This was back when a "floppy disk" really was floppy enough to manipulate in this way.)

Actually, there are probably dozens, if not hundreds, of different uses for a paper clip besides holding sheets of paper together. Are there 100 different uses for your product or service that you may not have considered before? Before you dismiss this possibility, keep in mind that you don't need 100 to boost your sales. You just need one.

Another example. Baking soda is for cooking, right? Well, it can be . . . but for some strange reason the Arm and Hammer people insist on running these ads promoting its use as a refrigerator deodorizer. By the way, do you know anyone who uses baking soda that way now?

Sometimes thinking creatively about your product or service means transcending the limits of what the end user is "supposed" to do. For instance, we all know you're not supposed to play with your food. Or are you? The people at General Foods think you should. They make Jell-O (and about 1,000 other successful consumer products). Some years back, General Foods launched a huge media campaign that was intended solely to familiarize consumers with the idea of making Jigglers—cookie-cutter shapes—out of gelatin, then letting the kids play with the Jell-O before devouring it. They gave away the Jiggler molds for free with any Jell-O purchase. An informal study of the market results (i.e., me watching what the people in front of me in line have brought to the checkout counter) yielded the admittedly unscientific observation that a lot more people than usual seemed to be buying Jell-O and buying it six, eight, or even twelve packs at a time. That's product malleability.

Take a good look at what your company offers its customers. Does what you sell work in only one way? Or can you adjust it? Can you make it serve some new purpose or function? Can you present it in a different light, or to a different group of people?

I'm not saying you have to develop an elaborate list of entrepreneurial ideas (although it probably won't hurt your sales career if you do). Keep things simple to begin with if that's what you prefer. Start with just one variation. If it's a winner, you may very well find that it can change not only your career in sales—but perhaps also change the very business in which you operate!

Closings and Openings

Meeting with a new prospect? Don't get distracted with thoughts of how you're going to *close* the deal with this person. Focus instead on the seven premeeting steps that will help you *open* the relationship effectively. If you do this for every new prospect you meet, you'll find that your overall closing numbers will improve.

Step one: Practice answering the question, "What do we sell?" You must be able to *concisely* describe the products and services your organization offers—and how, specifically, those products and services benefit your company's customers.

Step two: Practice answering the question, "What makes us different from the competition?" Your prospect may well have one and only one way of distinguishing potential vendors (say, price). You should be familiar with all the differences between yourself and the organizations you're competing against, and be ready to discuss them.

Step three: Practice answering the question, "What makes us better than the competition?" Be prepared to explain, briefly and enthusiastically, why someone should buy from you, rather than someone else. If you're not comfortable doing this, you're in the wrong job! Take the initiative. Do the research. Find out *why* your company's #1 client decided to buy from you, rather than anyone else.

Step four: Be prepared to complete the sentence, "Even though we're not always the least expensive option, people buy from us because . . ." The response you come up with may sound like this: "Well, the reason ABC Company decided to go with us, even though we weren't the lowest-priced option, was . . ."

Step five: Do the right pre-meeting research. Once you've scheduled a face-to-face meeting, it's time to do a little digging. Use the Internet and other resources to learn about the prospect's organization. In addition to checking out the target company's World Wide Web site, you should ask other people within your company about sales opportunities that may exist in accounts like this—opportunities that you may not know about. And while you're at it, you should also identify at least three of your company's success stories that are likely to be of interest to this specific prospect.

Step six: Create the flow. In other words, decide how you're going to open the meeting. You could say, for instance, "Would it help if I went first?"—and then offer a short "commercial" for yourself and your company, followed immediately by a question about what the other person does. This is a critical point in the meeting. What is the first question you'll ask? Why? What are likely to be the most appropriate follow-up questions? How will you phrase them? Remember—the sales process is an extended conversation, and we can use effective questions to control the flow of that conversation.

Step seven: Establish your Next Step strategy. What do you want to happen at the end of the meeting? We believe you should always try to get some tangible, scheduled commitment for action from the prospect—a Next Step. Decide on your primary Next Step strategy—say, another meeting with the same person a week from tomorrow at 2:00 to review a preliminary proposal. Decide, too, on at least one *backup* Next Step you can ask for, just in case you don't get your primary Next Step. For instance, you might ask for the chance to meet with the prospect's team, interview them, and report back with your findings.

Why are these seven steps so important? Because they help you keep your priorities straight. They keep you focused on the person who really matters: the prospect. Just as important, perhaps, they help keep you from trying to close the sale the minute you walk in the door.

Focusing on "closing" the deal instead of "opening" the relationship is a classic sales mistake. Whenever people contact our company to ask whether we have a strategy that will help them improve their "closing skills," we know there's already a problem. If someone is focused on improving a sales staff's "closing techniques"—on the staff's ability to say some mysterious set of magic words that will get people to buy—then we know there's really a diagnosis issue, not a "closing" issue. Specifically, we know that the person we're talking to is focused, in an unproductive way, on the *end* of the sales process, rather than on what comes *before* the close—the part where we find out about the prospect. That early portion is arguably the most important part of the sales relationship!

Ideally, we want the prospect to *decide* to buy; we don't want to have to "sell" to the prospect at all. In fact, "closing" is just another word for what happens when someone decides, on their own, to *use* what we have to offer. We can't force anyone to do anything. Well, before the prospect can make that decision to *use* our product or service, we should make some kind of a recommendation—a recommendation that makes so much sense to the prospect we're talking to that that person *will in fact* decide to buy from us.

So . . . what should that "makes sense" recommendation be based on? It should be based on information we've gathered from the prospect, of course. In fact, we want to spend *most* of our time with the prospect gathering information, so we can prepare that recommendation that "makes sense." Now, in order to make that information-gathering phase as productive as possible, we must prepare properly for the *very first meeting*—the meeting where we establish rapport, open up the relationship, and begin the all-important process of asking questions about what the other person is actually doing.

The seven pre-meeting steps you've just learned are, I believe, what make high closing ratios possible. Follow them!

CHAPTER 11

Don't Overwhelm
the Prospect

In the sales cycle we reviewed earlier, there is often a temptation on the part of the salesperson to jump from the second to the third stage before it's time to do so.

We walk in the door, shake the prospect's hand, engage in a little small talk, sit down when the prospect invites us to sit down, and then panic. It's time to start talking about something, and we're not exactly sure what that is, so we lay all of it, every bit, on the person sitting behind the desk.

When our company was founded. What model equipment we offer. Our complete list of past clients. The voltage required to run the equipment successfully in Europe. Recent design changes. Our company's sterling fourth-quarter results. How many drafts the president's message in our most recent annual report went through. What color tie the president was wearing when he had his picture snapped for that annual report.

And it just keeps coming out like that.

In my seminars, I refer to this phenomenon as "throwing up on the prospect." Yes, you read right, it's called "throwing up on the prospect," as in "regurgitating." We regurgitate any and every fact about our product or service we can think of, because we are so intimidated by the prospect of actually doing what we've come to do—namely, *listen* to the prospect—that we feel that, at least if we're talking, we must be doing something right. Oh, sure, we stop for breath once in a while and remember that someone told us a long time ago that the key to success in sales is getting the prospect to talk; so we ask a question of dubious relevance. Then when we get the answer we say something like, "Wow, I'm glad you told me that, because we've been able to help umpty-ump customers with a similar problem" and we get back to the task at hand: listening to ourselves talk.

After all, we've read somewhere that you're supposed to repeat, repeat, repeat. Because the prospect's kind of dumb, you can't count on the prospect understanding if you explain just one time. You have to say it twelve times. So that's what we do. And in the process we steamroll the person we are supposed to be learning about. Having asked the prospect a few questions, we resume throwing up. And then we try to schedule an appointment for a presentation, and boy, oh, boy, do we expect that presentation to close. Because we've done all the groundwork. We've told 'em and told 'em what we told 'em. Let 'em talk for a nanosecond or two. And told 'em again.

All too often, we try to rush this all-important second stage, and the result is, we tell the prospect everything on earth *except* how what we've got to offer will help solve *his or her unique problems.*

And the reason we can't do that is that *we don't know what those problems are.*

Hey, it works for everybody else on the customer list, right? How different can this company be?

Well, as it turns out, that's exactly the question you're supposed to be able to answer at the end of the interview stage. How different *can* this prospect be?

Find out the answer. Don't throw up on your prospect. Listen.

Selling to Committees

Too many sales are lost because salespeople don't know how to sell to—and close—committees.

Let's take as our starting point the idea that you must be *in front of the committee in the first place* if this is the setting in which your proposal will be discussed and have its fate decided. You must make your presentation to that committee if you want to influence the decision in your direction!

I can't tell you how many times I've had conversations like the following with salespeople who come to my seminars.

> *Me:* So who's making the decision in this account? Is it Ms. White, your contact?
>
> *Salesperson:* Oh, no. I'm talking to her, but the decision's being made by the finance committee.
>
> *Me:* Why don't you make your presentation to the finance committee, then?
>
> *Salesperson:* I can't just make a presentation to the finance committee. They're a committee. They meet and decide things. They don't want me there.
>
> *Me:* Have you tried asking Ms. White if you could make a presentation at one of their meetings?
>
> *Salesperson:* Well . . . no.
>
> *Me:* Try it.

Salesperson: You mean, just come right out and ask her whether or not I can sit in on a finance committee meeting and make a presentation?

Me: Right.

Salesperson: Can you *do* that?

Of *course* you can ask to make a presentation at a committee meeting!* And you know what? More often than you probably expect, you'll get the opportunity to state your case. And you know what else? More often than you probably expect, you'll close the sale! (Let's face it: many of these meetings are awfully dull. My theory is that you'll often get the business simply in appreciation for having livened things up.)

Remember, now, we're talking about *presentations*—what you do after you've learned *everything* you need to know about the prospect company. One key for successful presentations to committees is persistent professionalism—the ability to convey at all times that you understand the world of business, and, specifically, the function of the *prospect's* business: turning a profit.

Another key for successful presentations to committees is to identify *early on and to everyone's satisfaction* exactly what you're there for. You want to know that every single person in that committee room agrees with the basic premise as to *why* you're meeting with the group. Don't assume that everyone in the room knows what your main contact knows. Be prepared to lay some groundwork. One technique I like to use is to set up a sharp-looking sheet that I can circulate to all members of the committee, outlining what my main contact and I have established so far.

---

*In fact, you should also ask to set up the next step *before* you walk in: "What I'd like to do is attend the meeting, and then, following that, I think you and I should get together. Why don't we schedule that now?"

You might begin your presentation by passing out such a sheet, giving people time to review it, and then saying, "Here are the objectives as we understand them at my company. Before we start in on the presentation, can I ask if there are any questions or comments about your company's objectives as I've summarized them here?" If necessary, review your sheet point by point, asking each time whether there is agreement to what you've put forth. Often, there will not be. Better to know this now than during the heart of your proposal! At least now you can adjust your approach somewhat.

Listen to what people say. Take notes.

As you proceed through the presentation, stopping for questions wherever appropriate, you'll get a better idea of how your solution may or may not be able to work at this organization—and you'll also get a better idea of the internal politics of the committee. If you feel things are going your way, and you sense that your ideas have been examined and found promising, you may decide to try to close then and there by saying something like, "Well, that's what we have to offer. And I have to tell you, it sounds good to me. How does it sound to you?"

It's *easier* to assume (without evidence) that you can't meet with the entire committee. But it's more expensive. It will cost you the sale.

(And by the way, this advice also applies to sales that *don't* depend on a committee, but on a single decision maker "at the top." How many salespeople have assumed that they would not be allowed to present to this person—and simply present at a lower level? You must meet with the *person or persons who will be making the ultimate decision about your product or service*—even if it takes a long time to track that person down!)

As you will find as you continue through the book, there are any number of variations on that standard close. But what I've just outlined is the basic approach that I—and many,

many, many salespeople who've taken my seminars—have used with success in dealing with committees.

Preparing for the Meeting

How should you prepare for a meeting with a committee? Here are five points to keep in mind as you get ready for any sales-related meeting with a group of three or more at your target company.

1. Test the waters . . . by asking to help compose the agenda. News flash: People don't walk into committee meetings neutral. One good way to tell whether you've got active opposition to the purchase of your product or service is to see what happens when you try to a) help compose an agenda for the meeting, or b) place your topic near the head of an already-drafted agenda. If you get resistance on either front, it's a good bet you've got more alliance-building to do before the meeting takes place. Remember that one great way to kill an initiative without opposing it openly is to place it near the bottom of an agenda, so that it is never addressed, or only addressed at the very end of a meeting (and thus more likely to be "postponed for future discussion.")

2. Try to connect ahead of time with the person who formed the committee in the first place. This person may not even be on the committee at all—yet he or she may well be the final decision maker when it comes to purchasing your product or service. Granted, it may take a little effort and diplomatic skill to find some way to connect with this individual (and keep your primary contact happy), but the potential reward more than

justifies the calls you'll make. Ask, "What do you think the main concerns of the committee will be?"

3. Try to connect ahead of time with key players on the committee. If you don't know who they are, ask your main contact. If that approach doesn't yield any meaningful information, try doing the research yourself. You can at least get a vague idea of who's involved by asking your contact how many good copies of your agenda and materials you'll need to create. Then ask if you can send these documents along ahead of time so you can get "a little feedback" before the meeting. Again, ask, "What do you think the main concerns of the committee will be?" Try to get a sense of what the outcome of the meeting is likely to be. After all, the participants are likely to know the outcome ahead of time. Why shouldn't you?

4. Set the next step before the meeting. After you make your little presentation, there will probably be no immediate decision. People will need to "talk things over" and "confer." That's fine. But sales is all about momentum and interaction, so be sure to set your post-meeting appointment with your main contact *before* you actually step in the door. It could sound like this: "Why don't you and I schedule a time right now to meet on Friday?" (This assumes "Friday" is two days after the meeting, and that you're making the request two days *before* the meeting.)

5. Don't always swing for the fences. Identify what, precisely, you want the committee to authorize—and think twice before you make the deal a huge one. The most experienced salespeople learn quickly that there are times when it makes sense to ask for a relatively modest commitment, even if the presentation went extremely well. This can be an especially important

point if the prospect is an extremely large organization. Sometimes the "major deal" that seems to arise from a superb presentation to a committee at a big company ends up getting bogged down for months while everyone on earth "reviews," "discusses," "shares concerns," and (worst of all) "checks with Legal." Personally, I'd rather get a firm initial commitment on something small—a pilot program or a test shipment—and expand it slowly from there.

Understanding Responses .

If you've been selling for any significant amount of time, you're already familiar with the syndrome.

You're in the middle of a face-to-face meeting with the prospect. You're asking questions and gathering information, or perhaps even giving a presentation, having moved along somewhat in the sales cycle. Suddenly your prospect turns to you and asks you some bullet-nosed, steel-plated question seemingly designed to blow you out of the water. (Note, please, that I said *seemingly;* in actual practice the prospect is only using this abrupt approach to sound out potential problems, and probably isn't even thinking in terms of whether or not you're in the water.) The question could sound something like one of these:

- *Who have you worked with before?*
- *Do you tend to work with small or large firms?*
- *What kind of dollar volume did you post last year?*
- *Is this stuff guaranteed?*
- *How many clients in my industry have you worked with?*

And so on. And as you hear the question roll across the desk, something in you says, "Run."

You feel as though it's going to be impossible to answer the query and keep the cycle moving forward. And, sure enough, once you take your deep breath and give your best, straight-in-the-eye, honest response, you hear something along these lines:

- *Oh, this isn't really what we're looking for.*
- *We don't work like that.*
- *I don't think this is going to be a good match.*
- *This isn't going to be right for us.*
- *I'm afraid I may have been wasting your time; I don't think you're the kind of firm we're likely to work with.*

Salespeople have lots of different names for these kinds of remarks. Some people call them objections—I prefer to think of them as responses, or issues.

Whatever you call them, they're something most of the salespeople I train don't like. In actuality, though, we should welcome these responses. They tell us that the prospect is actually listening and thinking about our products or services. These exchanges give us the opportunity to advance the sale by overcoming them when that's appropriate. Whether we overcome them or not, we gain insight into what the prospect is considering.

It's important not to respond too quickly to an issue. Often, we hear a negative response and *assume* that it's a major roadblock (especially when it concerns price). This is not always the case.

A word of caution: The most common reason people *don't* buy is that they see no need to change the status quo. You may be used to thinking of a particular company or group of companies as your "competition." In reality, your competition is the status quo—whatever the person was doing before you came along!

(Note: For more on handling responses, see also Chapter 20 and Chapters 23 through 25.)

The Big Secret

The secret to closing your sales is to use the early part of the cycle—the interviewing stage—to unearth the significant objections (or at least the vast majority of them). In the third section of this book, you'll learn that that means you will use the ideas that appear in this chapter *well before you make a formal presentation.* You read right! My system says, if you are consistently getting objections during the final stages of the sale, you're not doing it right!

Taking Responsibility

In my book *The 25 Sales Habits of Highly Successful Sales-people* I discuss a technique for rescuing a blown presentation that has worked for me more times than I can count. I've taught it for years in my seminars and one-on-one training sessions and gotten nothing but positive reactions. This book would not be complete if I didn't tell you about it.

I call the method "taking responsibility." I know that may sound like a novel idea at first, because it's so easy to let someone else—the company, the production department, whomever—assume responsibility for the ultimate happiness of the customer or prospect. But I think if you stop to reconsider, you'll probably realize that your best customers now have come to rely on you in an important way, and that much of your relationship with these kinds of customers is based on trust. Earning trust is really the same thing as accepting responsibility, and assuming personal responsibility for the sale as it progresses is a remarkably effective sales tool. It works so well that, if you're like me, the first time you hear about the technique, you'll probably wonder why you didn't incorporate it into your sales routine long ago.

Convictions

So how does it work? Well, to begin with, you have to be utterly, completely convinced in your own heart that you can offer your prospect the best possible solution to his or her problem. If that confidence isn't there, the technique I'm about to describe simply won't work. If the prospect (or anyone else) asks you to talk about your firm, you have to be able to reply with sincerity that you work for a one-of-a-kind, customer-first company and are proud to do so.

Now then. When you're on a sales visit, and you come to the closing stage, you simply say something along the lines of "It sounds good to me; how does it sound to you?" (Again, that may seem audaciously simple right now, but this method of closing will make more sense to you as you continue along in the book. For the sake of argument, however, the technique I'm outlining in this chapter can be adapted to just about any close.) One of two things is likely to happen. Either the prospect will answer your question receptively—and thereby start down the road to becoming a customer—or the prospect will back off and say "No" flat out. If you find yourself facing the second scenario, you take responsibility for whatever problem has arisen.

What do I mean by that? Well, at this point, the salespeople I know of who use this technique successfully are genuinely taken aback—even shocked. And it's no act. They believe in their company so completely, and know so much about the prospect by this stage of the game, that they are legitimately concerned to see any evidence of a negative response to the proposal they've made. And they state that concern in no uncertain terms. You can too.

What you say will sound something like this: "Mr. Prospect, I'm really not sure what to say. I am so convinced that we have the best service, the best pricing, the best customization, and the best reputation of any firm in our industry that I can think of only one reason for you not to sign on with us. And that's that I must have done something terribly wrong just now in giving my presentation. So I'm going to ask you to give me a hand, Mr. Prospect, and tell me where I went off course. Because, to be quite frank with you, I know this service is right for you, and I'd really hate to have made a mistake on something this important."

Getting the Information You Need

Wow! What do you think you'll hear in response? One thing's for sure. It's not going to be easy for the prospect to come back with a run-of-the-mill brush-off like, "It's just not up our alley, Susan." No, if you're Mr. Prospect, you probably respect the person who had the courage to say that to you, who believes so strongly in the service you're looking at. You're going to pass along information—information on exactly what the problem is with your firm's signing on.

In practice, you will find that the common response you'll hear after you take responsibility for the initial "No" will sound something like this: "No, no, no, Susan, it has nothing to do with you. It's on our end." And the prospect can then be expected to go into detail about the remaining obstacles. Then you have the facts you need to continue through the cycle.

Let me repeat: This can be a startlingly effective technique, but it requires absolute faith on your part that you can in fact deliver on your promises. There is another catch as well: You have to be willing to put aside the common fixation with "being right" we all share to a degree. But, hey, when it comes right down to it, would you rather be "right"—or close a sale?

Part Three

Rethinking Your Relationship with the Prospect

Write This Down

Yes, I really mean it. I want you to go get a piece of paper, or your sales notebook, or your call sheet, or whatever you use to write in your sales work. I want you to pull out the pen or pencil you always use. And I want you to copy the following sentence down verbatim.

You cannot force a prospect to do anything.

Believe me when I tell you that that sentiment is worth framing and hanging where you can see it every morning as you enjoy your coffee and doughnut.

When we try to force prospects into committing to actions they're not ready to take, *we lose.* The exchange becomes polarized. The prospect starts to worry about all the things that need to get done as soon as this uncomfortable meeting is over. We start to sweat. We start to worry. We start to push.

And we don't win the "middle-third" sales.

Now, even though you can't force your prospect to do any-thing, you certainly can find areas of *agreement* with your prospect! You certainly can highlight *potential solutions* for your prospect! You certainly can show things to your prospect that he or she may not have noticed before! And you can always act on areas of *mutual* opportunity with your prospect!

Your objective is to get the prospect to tell *you* what to do, or, at the very least, to work out a course of action on which you both are in complete agreement. If your aim is to intimidate, to overrun, to conquer, to pressure your prospect into fitting into your preconceived notion of how the two of you will work together, you should resign yourself right now to the fact that you are not going to achieve your full potential as a salesperson. In other words, you are not going to close sales you should close.

Everything that follows in this third section of the book depends on the sentence you just wrote down on that sheet of paper. Read it again right now! Read it every day!

CHAPTER 16

Four Categories

In your dealings with prospects and customers, you and your company will, whether you know it or not, be assigned one of four roles. The first three are what mediocre salespeople settle for. The last one is what salespeople who end up closing those "middle-third" sales on a regular basis set their sights on.

Role Number One: Seller

Lightning strikes. You happen to call someone who needs model X-43 widgets. (Or this person happens to call you.) You sell model X-43 widgets at a price that fits into the department's budget. Your contact has got a busy schedule and is at least six weeks behind on each of three incredibly complicated projects. One of them is that widget thing his boss keeps bugging him about. If he signs on with you, or anyone else who happens to offer roughly the same thing, he might be able to deliver things only five weeks late. You get the sale. (Three months later, however, your competitor calls and offers a "special deal." You lose the sale.)

Role Number Two: Vendor

You sell a company your widgets. A year passes without incident and the company puts you on the list of "current suppliers." There are lots of reorders. You get lots of commission checks. (Three months later, however, the CEO looks at a financial report, decides that it's time to "cut the fat out of the so-and-so department," and the widget acquisition budget is reduced by 68 percent. Since you have no contacts of any consequence at the company, you have no way to make your case. The following quarter, you're dropped as a supplier. You think a competitor of yours made a presentation somewhere in the organization. But you're not sure.)

Role Number Three: Supplier

You make a presentation to the VP of Production at a company. The VP likes what you have to say and makes you a supplier. When the word comes from on high to reduce widget acquisitions by 68 percent, you have lunch with the VP, make a good case, and get the top brass to keep widget acquisitions at 80 percent of last year's levels. (The following year, however, the VP's boss decides, for reasons you can't understand, to drop you like a hot potato.)

Role Number Four: Partner

After meeting with the board of directors of a customer of yours and outlining new ways in which the company can spend half as much money and use your widgets to do twelve new things that increase productivity in the organization, you get the sale. You convince the board to work with you as its sole supplier. Working with top people in the organization, you develop new and creative ways to make things happen with your widgets, things none of your competitors have even thought of yet. You're part of the planning process.

Take a Look at Your Own Customers

Having reviewed these four categories, take a look at your current list of customers right now. Granted, you probably can't expect to turn every single one of your customer relationships into partnerships. But you can certainly have a good idea where you currently stand. And the beautiful thing about the four categories is that a customer at the first level can be transformed into a customer at the second level; the customer at the second level can be transformed into a customer at the third level; and the customer at the third level can be transformed into a customer at the fourth level.

How many of your current customers would consider you a seller? A vendor? A supplier? Are there any that consider you a partner? If not, it's time to work to change that!

CHAPTER 17

Your Two Objectives for Your First In-Person Meeting

You've made the call. You've gotten the appointment. You're walking into the prospect's office for the first time. What is it, exactly, that you're trying to accomplish?

As it happens, there are two goals you should bear in mind as you initiate the first person-to-person contact.

Goal Number One: To send concise but unmistakable symbols of professionalism and accountability. To offer, in short, a brief self-identification message that *avoids the trap of self-obsession,* and that sends without any countervailing signals the message, "It is good business to do business with us."

Goal Number Two: To *listen.*

Note, please, that presenting the product or service is *not* a goal at this stage of the sales cycle! You don't know enough yet about your prospect's problems to propose a solution to them.

Back to the Definition of Sales

Do you remember how we defined sales a little earlier in this book? We said it was *asking people what they do, how they do it, when they do it, where they do it, why they do it, and who they do it with—and then helping them do it better.* That's precisely what you should begin to do in your first meeting.

That doesn't mean you *manipulate* your conversation with the prospect. It means you artfully *steer* that conversation into areas of mutual opportunity.

In my book *Cold Calling Techniques (That Really Work!),* I talk a little bit about how to engage the prospect in this way. Actually, though, the first in-person meeting is the more typical setting for this exercise in steering the conversation. Let's look at an example of how it might work *after the appropriate small talk necessary to ease the transition into "appointment-speak."* (This usually consists of making some complimentary remarks about the prospect's office, wall decorations, or the like; it may, however, be perfectly acceptable for you to mention a recent visit with a customer that has left you feeling excited and optimistic. How this initial phase is managed can vary a great deal depending on the industry in which you're working and the person you're talking to.)

In the sample dialogue that follows, notice how we send the "good-business-to-do-business-with-us" message early on, and then gently steer the prospect toward the questions regarding the past, the present, and the future. By the way, in all such encounters, you should always be sure to *take written notes* based on the information you get from your prospect.

> *You:* (after engaging in small talk) Mr. Prospect, would it
> help if I told you about me and my company first?
> *Mr. Prospect:* Yeah, why don't you do that.
> *You:* Okay. We've been in business for the last six months
> (two years, ten years, 200 years, whatever), and we
> happen to be the most dynamic widget company in the
> country. We've worked with companies like ABC
> Financial, DEF Communications, and GHI Printing,

and we've worked with each of them to develop a customized widget system that worked for their specific needs. Today I was wondering if we could talk a little bit about your company's widget plans.

Mr. Prospect: Shoot.

You: Okay. Have you ever worked with a widget company before?

Mr. Prospect: Well, yes, once we did, back in 1979.

You: How did it work out?

Mr. Prospect: Hmm . . . I can't recall any problems with it whatsoever, to tell you the truth. A couple of years after that, of course, we had some budget cutbacks; you know how it is . . .

You: So presently you're not using anything in this area?

Mr. Prospect: That's right. It comes up every now and then at board meetings, but there never seems to be enough of a reason to reconfigure the entire department's production equipment. So it usually gets tabled. My feeling is that a good widget system here could be worth looking at, though.

You: Okay. Now, I'm curious. Does your production department foresee about the same level of work in the next six to twelve months as it's doing right now? Or more? Or less?

Mr. Prospect: Funny you should ask about that. I was just talking to Roger Gardner over in production this morning, and he's a little concerned about how they're going to meet the targets for the next two quarters.

And given that information, you should continue to steer the conversation into the specific *hows* and *whys* of the situation at Mr. Prospect's production department. To give the most obvious example, you should, if you are meeting with someone who is using your competitor, Low Rent Widgets, ask, "Why did you decide to sign on with Low Rent?" The answer you get will tell you how your prospect *views* the decision to work with your competitor, and will probably shed light on the decision-making process. (If your contact has no idea why or how the decision was made to work with Low Rent, odds are you are talking to someone who is not directly involved in the decision to buy what you have to offer. Your objective then becomes to find out who *is* handling that decision, and you should try to enlist your prospect as an ally in that effort.)

Suppose you do, and suppose you get all the information you need. What's next? Well, I can tell you one thing; you certainly don't launch into a presentation during this first meeting!

So what *do* you do? The answer's in the next chapter.

CHAPTER 18

The Option at the End of the First Visit

At a moment that feels appropriate near the conclusion of your first meeting you can say something like this:

> *You:* Mr. Prospect, based on what you've told me here today, there are a number of ways we can work on this. I could take some time and develop some ideas about how your organization could benefit from what we have to offer, and then meet with you and your people again next week. How's next Tuesday at 2:00?

Notice what you've done. You've prepared for "a number" of options, but you have only presented *one*—namely, that you stop in again for a meeting so you can talk about your outline. (See Chapter 20.) If the prospect says this sounds like a great idea, schedule the appointment (before you leave the building—don't "call later and set things up"), get back to your office, and start preparing for next week. If the prospect doesn't seem ready to commit to this yet, you're still in a good position; there are other options to talk about. These might include meeting with other people in the organization to gather more information, providing appropriate samples or endorsements, or even inviting the prospect to spend some more time with you at an upcoming conference or company event at which he or she can learn more about what you have to offer.

If the prospect is unresponsive to any of the options you outline (and you should probably offer no more than three at this point in the relationship), you may want to go back to the beginning, by saying something like this:

> *You:* Mr. Prospect, I'm sorry, did I miss something a little earlier on when you were talking about reducing costs in the second quarter? How did you see your widget use fitting into that?

In other words, highlight one of the objectives Mr. Prospect has detailed for you during the interview, and, while assuming responsibility for misunderstanding that objective, tie your product or service to it. (As you may have noticed, this is a small-scale version of the "taking responsibility" approach to rescuing a presentation that goes haywire. In this abbreviated form, it is appropriate for use during this early phase of the sales cycle.)

If you still receive negative signals from your prospect, you are either talking to the wrong person in the organization, or dealing with an organization that is unlikely to benefit from what you have to offer.

Do not present your product or service if you are still in the second—interviewing—stage. You are not ready to do so!

CHAPTER 19

A Horror Story

I want to use this chapter to impress upon you the importance of actually *gathering information* during the interview stage. I want you to understand that by doing so, you will do two very important things.

First of all, you will gain invaluable information that will help you tailor your presentation to the prospect's needs.

Second of all, you will automatically stand out from just about every other salesperson the prospect encounters.

It's true. The vast majority of your competitors *don't really want to hear* about what the prospect does. They want to close and move on to the next one. They fool themselves into believing that all prospects they meet are identical, and they try to impose their solutions in exactly the same way, time after time.

Let me tell you a horror story. At least, it was a horror story to me.

Not long ago, we needed a new telephone system at my company. Because I'm a sales trainer, and because I want to learn as much as I can about how salespeople operate in the real world, I scheduled every appointment I could. We must have seen representatives from a dozen or more companies. (Of course, I also wanted to select the very best system I could!)

Now, I have to tell you something about my office. When you sit down across from my desk, there's a phone staring you in the face. That's right—I have two phones on that desk, one meant for me and one meant for whoever's sitting across from me. The reason? Well, when I train my own salespeople to do telephone work, I've found that I get the best results if I'm able to pick up and hear both sides of the conversation, and then critique afterwards. So there's a phone for me and a phone for whomever I'm training.

As I mentioned, we must have seen a dozen different sales reps. Some of them were more accomplished than others. Some of the systems were better than others. Most of the sales reps made at least the pretense of taking notes and asking about my company's needs.

And every single one of those reps sat across from my desk, in the chair that had the phone in front of it.

Ready for the scary part? Not one of them asked me why I had the phones arranged in this unusual way.

Can you imagine what would have happened if one of them *had* asked? (Besides me falling out of my chair from surprise, I mean.) They might have found out how I trained my salespeople! They might have learned something about the way I use telephones in my business! They might have gone on to ask *how many* salespeople I train in this way, or whether I had plans to expand to new cities! And who knows? They might even have been able to formulate a way for me to accomplish my training more effectively by setting the phones up differently!

But none of that happened. Because nobody asked. Nobody wanted to know what made my work different. (In the end, of course, I had to *instruct* the phone supplier we selected on how to set up the extra phone.)

Stand Out

Be the one-in-a-million salesperson. *Listen.*

Ask what the prospect plans to do with your product or

service. Ask about any unusual features or applications that seem to be part of the equation. Ask about what worked the last time the prospect tried this. Ask about what *didn't* work the last time the prospect tried this. Ask what the prospect's aims are a few years down the line.

Ask about anything and everything relevant to the way your prospect uses or would use your product or service to do the job. *Listen* to the answers you get, and *write them all down.*

Your prospect will begin to believe that miracles really do happen.

CHAPTER 20

Verifying Your Information

How many times has it happened to you? You're deliriously happy; you leave an initial meeting with a prospect, convinced that you've got a "live one." You tell your sales manager about the great meeting you had. You tell your colleagues about the great meeting you had. You call your grandparents and tell *them* about the great meeting you had.

Then you head back for the appointment you scheduled with that "live" prospect of yours—and suddenly things aren't so lively.

Even though the prospect looked you in the eye and told you he was interested during your last meeting, your presentation goes nowhere. The prospect tells you he or she "has to think about things." You leave the building dejected.

What happened?

You didn't verify your information, that's what happened. You found out the hard way that when people *say* they're interested in what you have to offer, that's not necessarily the same thing as their actually *being* interested in what you have to offer.

You feel lousy. You didn't realize how much you had invested in this sale—not just in terms of time, but also in terms of your emotions. It takes you some time to get back on track. You lose a little bit off your fastball.

How do you keep from wasting time and energy being

ecstatic and rejected, ecstatic and rejected, over and over and over again? How do you identify those prospects who really aren't going to buy from you no matter what you do? I'll show you in this chapter. If you follow the simple advice you find here, you'll learn how to spot nonstarters from your prospect base and focus on the people who really represent your prime selling opportunities. And, if your results are anything like those of the people I train, you'll end up closing 80 percent of the people you *do* focus on.

Get Serious

What I'm about to suggest that you do takes courage, but you will save yourself a lot of time, effort, and aggravation if you do it.

At the conclusion of your interviewing phase—whether that is at the end of the first meeting or the end of the fifth meeting—say something like this:

> *You:* Mr. Prospect, I think we've had a very productive meeting here, and I've certainly learned a lot about your organization. But I don't think I'm ready to put together a full proposal for you yet, and I have to say, I want to spend a little time so that I can put together some ideas on this. If you don't mind, I'd like to go back to my office and work up an outline of the ways we can help you, and then meet again here next week, so we can talk about that before we give you a formal proposal.

Set the time, then go back to your office and work up your outline. Note that your next meeting will *not* be the presentation of a formal proposal!

An alternative to the above is to ask the prospect to schedule a meeting with you and a higher-up (say, the president, or perhaps your own sales manager) from your organization. Whatever you do, come back with a written outline of what you can do for the prospect, with rough estimates of time commitments and prices. This outline will differ from a full-fledged proposal in two important ways. First, it does not offer final time estimates and prices. Second, you want the prospect to object to it.

That's right. You want to get the "wait-a-minute, how-much-did-you-say" feedback at this point—and not when you're making your formal proposal. And remember, you're in no hurry. You can take as many meetings as is necessary to verify your information.

After you pass along your outline and have given the prospect the chance to review it, you might say something like this:

You: Mr. Prospect, as you can see, I've used this outline to review what seemed to me to be the most important points from our last meeting. If you don't mind, I'd like to go over them with you now, so that I'm absolutely positive I understand what you're saying. If I heard you right, your main objectives are, number one, to increase the performance rate of your salespeople by increasing their gross dollar volume by at least 15 percent over the next three months; number two, to reduce the amount of time your salespeople spend dealing with unproductive accounts; and number three, to keep your training expenses this quarter beneath the $20,000 figure that shows up in your budget. Does that sound like an accurate description of what we talked about last time?

Important! Do not attempt to "verify information" by repeating what *you've* said during the interview stage. (In other words, don't launch into a monologue about how wonderful you and your product are.) Verify the information you've gotten from the prospect! What this means is that the verifying stage should *never sound the same twice,* because each prospect is unique. If you're planning to use this technique as an opportunity to talk about what *you* do, how many other customers *you've* helped, what kind of success record *you've* posted, you might as well not bother.

Let the prospect correct you, and listen to all those corrections. That's how you get the correct information you need to make your presentation.

If you've really been listening, and if your prospect has been dealing openly with you, after you summarize the key points of the interview you will hear something along these lines:

Prospect: Yes. I think you've isolated the big points we're interested in.

Or:

Prospect: Gee, the price seems a little high.

If you meet with resistance from your prospect at this point, ask where you have misunderstood the prospect's goals, *take notes,* and repeat the process of summing up the key points and asking for confirmation. In other words, *involve the prospect* in the process of drafting your proposal. Take the objections head-on *now,* not at the presentation stage. (For more ideas on dealing with obstacles at this point, see Chapter 13.)

Once your prospect agrees that you have a good

understanding of the goals involved, I want you to say something like this:

> *You:* Great. Now, Mr. Prospect, I want to ask you something here that's pretty important. If I go back and use this outline to develop a proposal specifically for your company, based on what we've talked about here today, and if that proposal addresses all the issues we've identified and puts you in the position of being able to expect to achieve those three goals, could you see yourself working with us on this?

After you say that, *stop talking* and listen to what your prospect has to say. You've asked a fair question; you're entitled to a straight answer.

If you get a positive response (not necessarily an unqualified "Yes, we'll work with you," mind you, but something along the lines of "If the proposal meets all three of those objectives, then yes, I think we'd seriously consider it") then schedule the meeting *then and there* and set up your customized proposal. At this point, the prospect should know that you intend to try to close at the end of your presentation.

If you *don't* get a positive response, say thank you, ask if you can call back again in a month or so just to check in and see how things are going, smile, shake hands, leave, and move on to the next prospect.

Hard medicine, I know, but it works. It really does deliver a closing rate from this point forward of *80 percent.* Isn't that worth shooting for?

You don't want to try to close unless you've developed the right proposal, and you won't have the right proposal unless the *prospect helps you write it.*

Similarly, you shouldn't waste your time developing proposals for people who don't really want to do business with you. *Listen* for the prospect's objectives, verify your information, and ask if there's a realistic chance that you and the prospect can do business together. You'll save a lot of time, and—added bonus—you'll actually *win* points for professionalism in the eyes of the vast majority of your prospects, no matter how they answer you. You'll let them know that you're not like every other salesperson who walks in the door—and believe it or not, they'll be relieved! What's more, you'll let people know that *you* know the value of your own time.

Please Read This

The verification technique you've just read about in this chapter is the heart of this system.

If you use it, you will see improved results in your closing efforts. (As I've pointed out, the students in my seminars report that, when they follow my advice, *including* the advice to let the prospect help you draft the proposal, they close at an 80 percent rate from that point forward!)

If you don't use this technique, you won't get the full benefit of this program.

Try what I've described. See what happens. I know you'll be happy with the results.

CHAPTER 21

What Is a Presentation?

A presentation is a summary of *how you can help the prospect do his or her job better, concluding in a specific timetable and a specific price.*

A presentation, in other words, contains real dollar estimates and real timetables, and is delivered to the right person.

A presentation is *based on the work you did in your interviewing stage.* Specifically, it's based on the information-verification technique you must use during your interviews. If you use the information-verification approach properly, you will identify and resolve the vast majority of your prospect's objections before you even begin your formal presentation.

A presentation is structured according to the specifics of your company and your industry.

A presentation is delivered both in writing and orally.

A presentation looks sharp in its written form, because you've put a lot of time into developing it and you've selected the best possible format for it.

A presentation sounds sharp because you've practiced delivering it ahead of time.

A presentation is not assembled until after you have developed the outline *with the person who will be making the final decision.*

A presentation is *delivered to the person or people who will be making the final decision.*

A presentation features a cover letter, an executive

summary (basically a one-page overview of what follows), body copy that outlines in detail what you plan to do for the organization, and, finally, a statement of cost.

A presentation is something your prospect *knows is going to conclude in your attempt to close.* (See the earlier chapter on verifying your information.) In fact, I like to begin my presentations by saying something like, "You know, we've worked really hard together on what we're about to talk about today. I have to tell you, having looked at all this information, I really believe we ought to work together. I think you'll think so, too."

A presentation is *unique*. It is, not surprisingly, tailored to the needs you've identified during your earlier discussions with the prospect. It's based on the prospect's objectives and concerns—not yours, and not those of any other customer you've worked with.

A presentation does *not* necessarily take place during your second face-to-face meeting with the prospect; depending on the organization you're trying to win as a client and the various concerns and political considerations associated with that organization, you may be in the interviewing stage for several meetings. (Indeed, it may take you a few meetings to even track down the people who should be answering your questions!)

A presentation is a *proposal that should lead to a decision on the client's part to work with you.*

A presentation is something *targeted toward a specific objective with a specific prospect.* Especially when trying to do business with a large firm for the first time, you should decide exactly what your aim is. Do you want to replace the current supplier? Or are you willing to accept a part of the business in the hopes of developing the relationship? Be realistic in your expectations, and, regardless of your decision, be honest about your selling objective with the prospect. Early on in the process, you might want to say something like, "Mr. Prospect, it's probably no surprise for you to hear me say that I very much want to work with your company. But you should know at the outset that I realize that you may feel some hesitation at working with a company our size. That's why I want you to know that I think it makes sense now for us to talk about how my company can help you with the widget reconfiguration aspects of your operation, rather than your entire widget acquisition plan. My objective is going to be to assemble a pilot program that we can re-evaluate in six months if you decide to work with us."

Be Sure to Incorporate Your Schedule

It bears repeating. Without a realistic timetable, you have not made a presentation. You have conducted a discussion about the two organizations; an enlightening one, perhaps, but a discussion and nothing more.

Your presentation should include a statement along these lines:

You: And, bearing all these obstacles in mind, we estimate that we will be able to do the job in three months. We propose beginning on the first of March and concluding on the first of June.

Be Sure to Incorporate Costs

Another mandatory content element of your presentation is a direct and unapologetic statement of the costs involved. The price estimate you develop should be based on your discussions with your prospect in the interview stage. If you don't ask the prospect about price during the interview stage, and instead incorporate a "fair" price that you expect the prospect to assimilate during your presentation, do not expect to close at that meeting! Expect to hear some variation on "I'll think about it."

Raising the issue of cost yourself—rather than waiting for the prospect to bring the issue up—allows you to take a leadership role. It also eliminates a frequent late-stage objection and keeps you from wasting time. (See Chapters 13 and 25 for detailed advice on price concerns.)

Remember your objective: to work with the prospect to develop a proposal that incorporates his or her concerns. You need to find out what price is going to work with your prospect (and determine what kind of negotiating room you have).

The verbal expression of your price estimate could sound like this:

> *You:* One of your aims was to keep the project under $45,000, due to third-quarter budget restraints. Our conclusion is that this is possible, and our price for the entire job would be $40,000, with half due on signing the contract and half due on completion.

Does your prospect know that you intend to try to close at the conclusion of the presentation?

This is the one that shakes everyone up at my seminars. Salespeople often say, "I don't know. I can't know, unless I talk to the prospect about it ahead of time." If you've read the chapter on verifying your information, however, you'll realize that talking to the prospect about your intentions is exactly what you *must* do.

What Next?

So much for the essentials of what the presentation *is*. There's a lot more to say, of course, about what happens after it's delivered, and we'll be examining that in the next chapters.

The Simple Closing
Statement, Revisited

This chapter is going to be a short one, because it has to do with what you need to say to begin the closing process.

If you've followed all the advice that we've been looking at, you should, at the conclusion of your presentation, be in the position to say something like this:

You: Mr. Prospect, I don't know about you, but this program makes a lot of sense to me. I think your company would benefit a lot from working with us. What do you think?

Breathtaking in its simplicity, isn't it? Here's a variation.

You: Mr. Prospect, we've spent a lot of time developing this together, and I have to tell you I have a good feeling about this. How do you feel about it?

If you're like most salespeople, a little light is beginning to glow in your head right about now. That light is glowing because you're realizing that if you do all the work up-front in the way that we've been discussing, if you work with the prospect to identify the most important goals, if you get the prospect's help in drafting the very proposal you will offer at the end of the sales cycle, then you probably *could* expect to close the sale using this absurdly simple statement!

Here's another version. By this point you should be quite familiar with how the basic idea can be adapted to your own selling environment and your personal selling style.

> *You:* Mr. Prospect, that's our proposal. I'll be very frank with you: It seems to me that we could really benefit from working together. What do you think?

Can you expect the prospect to smile, shake hands, and sign on at this stage? *If you've done your work properly,* that will happen a good portion of the time when you say this.

It won't, however, happen all the time. True, by working closely with your prospect you've probably isolated and resolved the vast majority of the objections you're likely to face well before you make the presentation, and well before you attempt to close. But what if, instead of those specific objections you faced earlier, you get (as is common enough) something a little more vague? What if you hear something like the ever-popular "Well, I'll have to think about it?"

Read on. We'll look at the "I'll have to think about it" problem in the next chapter.

CHAPTER 23

"I'll Have to Think about It"

If you hear "I'll have to think about it," or some variation on it, after you've made your presentation, say something like this:

> *You:* Well, Mr. Prospect, you know, as I finished this, I have to admit, I was a little concerned that I might have put too much emphasis on the (and here pick some *nonthreatening* aspect of your presentation). What did you think?

What you've done here is you've given the prospect the option to disagree with you. You've deliberately picked a relatively innocuous element of your sales presentation, and you've said to the prospect, "Hey, I made a mistake here, didn't I? Please correct me."

Nine times out of ten, if you've done your preparatory work correctly, and if you say something like the above, expressing your own concern that you may have put too much emphasis on the question of how to train the prospect's people to use your widgets, you'll hear something like this in response:

> *Prospect:* No, actually, it's not the training I'm concerned about. We've just got a problem with your specs.

I don't think the people out in Dubuque are going to be able to fit this into their production patterns.

You've uncovered the real obstacle! And from here you can work with the prospect to fine-tune what you have to offer. How do you get around it? Well, at D.E.I., we're very big on "parables"—in other words, we tell success stories. Stories are very powerful sales tools. If you can highlight an encounter with a particular customer of yours who *did* overcome the same or a similar obstacle, do so. If you don't know enough about your customers to be able to do this comfortably, *find out!*

If you encounter resistance along the lines of "I'll have to think about it" after you've made your formal presentation, *isolate a part of the presentation, express your concern to the prospect that you may have mishandled it, and ask for help.* In the vast majority of cases, the prospect will reassure you that what you've identified is *not* in fact the problem, and will say something like, "What we're really still thinking about is . . ."

Now, this approach should sound a little familiar to you. It's a subtler, more low-key version of the "taking responsibility" technique we explored earlier in the book. You may be tempted to use that technique in a more straightforward fashion when you hear "I'll have to think about it," but I'm going to suggest that you stick with the more laid-back approach I've outlined above. After all, as common as "I'll have to think about it" can be, and as frustrating as "I'll have to think about it" can be, it's really not the worst thing that can happen to you at this stage. You want to keep things moving ahead smoothly, and you certainly don't want to run the risk of polarizing the good working relationship you've worked so very hard to develop with your prospect.

So when *should* you use the "taking responsibility" method at full volume? That's the topic of our next chapter.

Dealing with Obstacles

Sometimes, of course, you'll encounter obstacles during your presentations. Typically, salespeople refer to these obstacles as "objections."

We really don't like the term "objections." It's better to think of them as responses. When someone tells you there's a problem with what you've proposed, that shows that the person is actually listening and thinking about your products and services. That means you have the opportunity to advance the sale by asking questions, by getting "righted," and then putting the spotlight on your organization's relevant resources.

Responses from the prospect give us the opportunity to gain insight on what the other person is thinking. Calling these responses "objections," on the other hand, sometimes changes the emotional atmosphere for the worse—and makes it harder for us to ask the right questions. Make no mistake: Asking the right questions is what it's all about at this stage. Somewhere along the line, things went awry. The question is, where?

By raising an issue—rather than flatly rejecting and refusing to discuss your recommendation—your contact is trying to draw your attention to something. Try to ask questions that will help you get to the bottom of whatever it is that the prospect is trying to get you to notice. Remember: *Any* feedback from the prospect is a form of "getting righted!"

As salespeople, we have to be extremely careful about the

assumptions we make when we encounter obstacles late in the sales process. Very often, we hear a negative response and assume that it is an objection, especially when it concerns price. In many cases, the prospect has simply raised an issue that needs to be explored. Sometimes what sounds like an "objection" about your payment terms is really a question about how much flexibility you're willing to show in invoicing. Sometimes what sound like rock-hard price concerns mask other issues, such as a need to be persuaded about your commitment to follow through and a desire to make sure that what you sell actually delivers the benefit you promise.

Price "objections" in particular should not be taken at face value. Let me give you an example of what I mean. Think about a time you bought an appliance, like a stereo or a television. What happened? Perhaps you walked into the store having decided that you wouldn't spend more than, say, $500. Perhaps you gave the store attendant a particular price range when asked about price, and perhaps he or she walked you over to a certain model.

What happened next? You probably found yourself bombarded with reasons why that particular model was just perfect for you. All the person has asked is how much you want to spend, and suddenly you've got this cascade of features coming at you, all apparently based on that one single piece of information: the price. Whatever intelligent interaction there was between you and the salesperson has stopped cold. If you're like me, you're quickly looking for reasons to *avoid* making a purchase commitment at this point.

Now think about what happens when you run into an *intelligent* salesperson in a retail setting, someone who's willing to ask you just a few questions about what you're doing, why you're doing it that way, and what you hope to do in the future. This kind of salesperson can often change your "I'm only spending $500" mindset into a "$750 seems worth it" mindset in a matter of minutes, and with very little effort. Haven't you had an experience like that before? I know I have!

The reality is, as salespeople, we often overreact when we hear what we think is a price objection. What we should be doing is getting to the bottom of the issue by asking intelligent questions *before* we commit to solving any problem the prospect raises.

For example, if the prospect says, "The pricing really isn't what I expected," we must fight the instinct to say, "Stop! Let me tell you why this is a great price!" or "I can ONLY cut it by 50 percent!" It might make more sense to explore the issue further by asking, "What kind of pricing were you expecting?" Your prospect might respond by saying, "Well, Joe told me he signed on with your company and paid less," or, "Well, I hadn't really thought about it at all." These are two totally different frames of reference! Step back and ask clarifying questions. Use appropriate success stories whenever you can.

Here are three simple steps for handling responses effectively:

1. IDENTIFY/ISOLATE the issues. Ask questions like, "What makes you say that?" or "Why that amount?" or "How does this concern fit into your goal of . . . ?"

    Then ask yourself: Do I really understand the problems my prospects typically face? What *is* this problem, really? (Never forget: Your prospect's initial assessment of an issue may be masking a deeper challenge.) Exactly how is this particular issue affecting this particular prospect, right now?

2. VALIDATE the issue. Figure out what its real-world dimensions are. Talk the challenge through openly and honestly with your prospect. (For instance: "You're not alone. My experience is that, if people have a

problem with our delivery dates, it usually comes up at this point in the discussion. Let's see what we can do.") Don't run away from the problem or pretend it doesn't exist. Offer appropriate additional information and help your prospect reach a logical conclusion.

3. RESOLVE the issue. This may be easier to do than you think. While every prospect is unique, accomplished salespeople tend to face the same half-dozen or so challenges over and over again within any given target industry. Don't use a cookie-cutter approach, but do share appropriate anecdotes and bring your personal and organizational experience to bear in developing a creative solution.

There are many different types of issues. Here are a few of the most common.

- *Problem/Question: "We used you a few years ago and had tremendous delivery problems."* There are easy and hard problems. The solution to an easy problem is to answer the question only and avoid reselling. For a hard problem, get help from an outside authority who can help you solve the issue.
- *Stall: "Let me run this by my people one more time."* Establish a timetable that works backward from the date of implementation, then articulate the steps that must follow—and determine a necessary decision date.
- *Reassurance: "With such a young sales force, this could be complicated to implement."* Build credibility. Ask the prospect how he or she was reassured previously about other vendors. Follow that approach, whether it means arranging for a letter of reference, a testimonial, a call to a current customer, or whatever.
- *Doubt: "How many people use this?"* and *Fear/*

Uncertainty: "Will this really work?" These responses have to do with a fear of change. The solution is to deal with the transition: Talk about how you will get the prospect started with your products/services and guide them through the initial stages. Take personal responsibility for the success of the program . . . and follow through!

Whatever you do, avoid instinctive, "knee-jerk" approaches to problems we *assume* to be present in the later phases of the sales cycle. Don't be like the telemarketer who called me recently, *closed the sale without any negative response whatsoever from me,* and then instinctively asked, "Do you need me to bring the cost down a little?"

What if I Get an Outright "No"?

"It's just not right for us."
    "I think we'll pass."
    "Thanks, but no thanks."
    Assuming you have followed my advice about developing your formal sales proposal in concert with the prospect, you should use the full-fledged "Mr.-Prospect-I'm-genuinely-surprised-please-tell-me-what-went-wrong" technique *only when you receive an outright "No."*
    This will be quite rare, but you should be prepared for it. And that "taking responsibility" technique I outlined in an earlier chapter is the perfect reaction to an outright, no-daylight rejection following your proposal. After all, if your prospect, after working with you to isolate all the issues and objectives, after telling you everything about his or her objectives in a given area, and after having told you to your face that it was likely that you'd close the sale if you hit all the points the two

of you identified together—if, after all that, the prospect can turn around and give you a flat "no," then you've got a *right* to be surprised. You've got a right to ask where things went wrong.

Remember, though, that the "taking responsibility" approach is predicated on your well-placed, unshakable confidence in your product or service. Remember that you are not supposed to be angry at the prospect, but expressing your (no doubt genuine) surprise. And remember that the aim of the technique is exactly what you tell the prospect your aim is: to find out where things went wrong so you can work from there!

CHAPTER 25

Money, Money

Recently, at a meeting with the top brass at a large bank, I was following my own advice and encouraging my prospects (in this case, it was a committee) to help me compose the proposal I would eventually present.

When it came to money (as it often does, either here or at a later stage of the sales cycle), I started getting funny signals. I'd talked about the plan I wanted to develop for the bank, I'd tried to identify the major objectives of the people I was working with, and I'd stated a *rough* (read: negotiable) dollar amount that was appropriate for the work I was anticipating doing. I said, "Let me give you a feeling for what I think this is going to cost." I named a figure. The president of the bank looked at me, smiled, and told me he had no problem with the amount of money I had mentioned. But the chief executive officer saw things differently.

He said to me, "I'm not sure that I want to pay that kind of money."

Because I'd been attentive during the interviewing stage, I knew that the company, although large and profitable, was growing fast, and was experiencing the kinds of cash constraints common in a high-growth environment. Companies that are growing rapidly tend to eat up a lot of cash. So instead of perceiving the chief executive officer's comment as a challenge to my program's viability, or as the first salvo in a negotiating war over my fees, I reacted to it *as though it were an expression of a concern about cash flow.*

Which, it turned out, was exactly what it was.

I offered the chief executive officer the opportunity to pay off my fee over an extended period, and he smiled broadly and said he thought that could work. A week later I made my presentation, asked the principals what they thought about what I had to offer, and closed the sale.

My point is not that you should always try to get around price obstacles by offering creative payment terms. *Sometimes* that will be the correct response; sometimes it won't.

My point is that, if you truly listen to your client, if you avoid the temptation to assume that *this* prospect's price objection is the same as the *last* person's price objection, you'll be in a much better position to get the information you need to put together a presentation that closes.

After all, can you imagine what would have happened in that case if I'd assumed that their financial situation was exactly like that of the last prospect I'd met with? If I'd held off discussing the issue of price until the very end of the process? I would have named a figure. The president would have said it made sense. The chief executive officer would have had his reservations. Everybody would have said that the committee needed time to think. I would have left. At some point the chief executive officer would have pointed to his (valid!) cash flow concerns, and someone could have pointed out, rightly, that I had not mentioned anything about any payment plans. The committee would have had to assume that I would require a standard half on signing, half on completion, and could have felt uncomfortable asking me for other terms—if they'd thought about asking at all. And I would have lost the sale!

CHAPTER 26

Some General Ideas for Closing Success

- Don't rush the sales cycle.
- Don't underestimate the importance of prospecting.
- Monitor your prospecting results. What are your ratios?
- Ask key people *what they're trying to accomplish* in the area in question. (When you do, you will automatically distinguish yourself from your competition.)
- If you're finding that, over and over again, you're losing sales because of the *same objection*—say, that your price is too high—you are probably facing some problem on an organizational level. Take the time to talk to your sales manager about your company's strategies and market position.
- Once you have made contact by telephone, build your first in-person visit upon your past discussion with that contact. Don't begin from scratch as though you'd never spoken with your contact before! If possible and appropriate, mention some memorable element or remark from the earlier phone conversation. This will move the prospect away from the "it's-time-to-talk-to-some-salesperson" mindset and toward the "this-is-that-interesting-person-from-that-interesting-company" mindset.

- Don't obsess on a single account. I worked with one woman who boasted that she had visited a single account thirty-three times before closing. That may sound impressive—but what if the time she spent on that call could have been devoted to prospecting efforts that would have led to *two* (or, quite possibly, considerably more) sales?
- Don't try to present during the interview stage.
- Don't confuse a *presentation* with a *demonstration*. The presentation is what you do after you've gotten all the information you need from the prospect during your interviewing stage. A demonstration of your product or service may take place much earlier; it's something you do to elicit interest at an earlier point in the sales cycle.
- Visit the prospect's manufacturing facility or other "real-world" environment.
- Encourage the prospect to visit your office.
- If your selling environment and industry are appropriate for it, consider using visual aids.
- Don't place too much emphasis on reams of reports, color brochures, or elaborate pie charts and regression analyses. Deluging the prospect with information is a common and costly mistake. As a general rule, prospects will have a hard time forming a positive view of anyone or anything when forced into information overload; salespeople usually ignore this and pile the paper on anyway.
- When you take notes, *take notes!* Don't take notes so the prospect will *think* you're taking notes! Take notes! (I once met with a telephone system salesperson who asked whether I'd mind if he took notes during our meeting. Of course, I said I had no problem. He pulled out a single crumpled piece of paper and a ragged, chewed-on ballpoint pen. As I told him what we were

looking for in our next system, he smiled and nodded and, over the course of the next half hour, wrote down *one thing* on that piece of paper. He wrote the number eight. That was how many lines there were in our office. What kind of proposal do you think he was able to put together based on notes like that?)

- Bear in mind that, by introducing price during the interviewing stage, you are relieving much of the pressure from the prospect. (For many prospects, you will probably be passing along the extremely valuable information that your service costs less than they think.)

- Don't place too much trust in media accounts about the objectives of your target company. The media are often wrong. Reading articles or watching television programs may be an important adjunct to your interviewing and verification efforts, but they can't replace them.

- Remember that you're working with an individual (or with a group of individuals), not an institution. You represent your company, yes—but your company isn't making the presentation, you are. Establish a relationship between two people, not two corporate entities. Tell your prospect that *you* want the business, not that your company does.

- Find out how decisions relating to purchasing your product or service have been made, or how decisions relating to similar purchases have been made. Odds are that the decision about your product or service will be made in essentially the same way. Specifically, if you learn that the decision has in the past always been made by a committee, *find a way to make your presentation directly to that committee*. Don't waste your time with a single member of the committee if you can possibly avoid it.

- If you and your prospect face a considerable gap in age or in some other aspect of your professional demeanor— if, for instance, you are a woman in your mid-twenties trying to close a dyed-in-the-wool "good old boy" in his mid-sixties who can't seem to bring himself to treat you as a professional equal—consider making your presentation with another member of your organization, someone who may be able to put your prospect at ease. (This "escalation" technique is also particularly effective when you're dealing with a prospect who needs reassurance that he or she is making the right decision.)

- Aim high; don't assume you can't make your presentation to the top person in an organization. Even if this person does not make the final decision regarding the product or service you have to offer, he or she can be a powerful ally. Try starting at the top and eliciting "power referrals" from the top people in your target organization.

- Be ready for common objections and don't be caught off-guard by obstacles that are common in your field. (If you think back, you'll probably recall that this has happened to you on a number of occasions. Many sales are lost when salespeople are surprised by prospect queries and comments that should really come as no surprise at all.)

- Keep your promises. People will remember you.

CHAPTER 27

The Leadership Role

Throughout the interviewing stage, and certainly before you reach the point at which you're ready to make a presentation to your prospect, you should solidify your image as a leader.

For many salespeople, this seems to get a little tricky, because, as you'll remember, your aim in the early part of the sales process is to get the *prospect* to talk to you about objectives and what they *do*. How, you may be asking yourself now, are you supposed to do that and get the prospect to see you as a leader?

Actually, there's no contradiction at all. Think back to the advice I gave you about handling the interviewing stage. I said that you should convey the message that it's good business to do business with you, and then steer the conversation in such a way that the prospect does the talking.

Yes, I said "steering." Steering a car means *driving* the car! Steering your conversation with the prospect means *driving* that conversation!

We often get hung up on definitions. Sometimes when we hear the word "leadership," we automatically think of people telling other people what to do. A real leader knows that if that's all you focus on, you're dead.

A leader *inspires.*

A leader *knows what he or she knows.*

A leader *does not try to hide what he or she doesn't know.*
(One of my favorite accounts of Dwight D. Eisenhower cites

the fact that, while he was acting as Supreme Allied Commander in Europe during World War II, Ike flabbergasted superiors and subordinates alike by admitting openly when he didn't know the meaning of technical terms.)

A leader *knows how to get the best out of the people with whom he or she works.*

A leader *adds value to just about everything he or she touches.*

A leader *makes people feel more important after meeting with them.*

A leader *points the way after studying all the angles.*

A leader *is accountable.*

A leader *takes the good with the bad with equanimity.*

A leader *keeps an open mind.*

A leader *sees opportunity even in a setback.*

A leader *seizes opportunity.*

A leader *knows when to trust instincts and when to ask for further information.*

A leader *isn't afraid of new ideas.*

A leader *knows that if good business relationships come first, money usually follows.*

A leader *knows that open dialogue is essential to true creativity.*

A leader *thinks in the long term.*

A leader *knows there is no point in burning bridges.*

A leader *doesn't have to cajole others into being truthful; they do it of their own accord.* (As a result, salespeople who are real leaders don't spend a lot of time worrying about whether or not they can trust the people they work with. Far, far, too many salespeople get trapped into the no-win situation of obsessing about whether or not the prospect has "misled" them. If that's the level at which things are operating, you might as well give up.)

A leader *takes a relatively long time to make a decision— and will generally stick with that decision, even in the face of obstacles.*

By the same token, a leader *knows when to try something new.*

How Do You Rate?

Many salespeople confuse leadership with manipulation. With rare exceptions, manipulators are not particularly good leaders because people have difficulty coming to trust them. It's tough to inspire people who don't trust you.

A disproportionately high number of top corporate executives were, at an earlier point in their career, highly successful salespeople. Doesn't that tell you something? Doesn't that tell you that there's something in the nature of what you're doing for a living that helps build bridges, and partnerships, and long-term alliances? Doesn't that tell you that solving the problems of others on a professional level has something important in common with the ultimate leadership role in an organization?

Throughout the sales cycle, you must project the professional image of the leader with your prospect. That doesn't mean you order the prospect around. (God forbid!) It means you take the time to hear the prospect's problems in their entirety—then bring to bear the full weight of what you have to offer in solving those problems. That way, when you finally do say, "Follow me," it won't be overbearing or sound like it's coming out of the blue. It will be the most natural thing in the world, because *you have a plan.* It should be obvious to you by now that, if you don't have a plan, you can't expect to be considered a leader.

But if you make the effort to develop that plan, if you do your homework, and if you incorporate the prospect's concerns every step of the way—you can say, with every right, "Follow me." And the prospect will follow you.

CHAPTER 28

Don't Reinvent the Wheel

You're nearly at the end of the book. The ideas I've described here have been simple—simple but revolutionary. And because they're revolutionary, they may be tough for you to think about implementing in your honest-to-goodness, real-life sales work.

Perhaps you're saying to yourself, "It all sounds great—but I'm not really sure it's the right thing to do for me, or for my industry, or at this company."

Don't let rationalizations rob you of winning those all-important "middle-third" sales. Give yourself the benefit of the doubt. Give this program a try for a good stretch of time—a month or two, say, or, at the very least, twenty-one days. (As you'll remember, that's the amount of time it usually takes to instill a good habit or eliminate a bad one.)

Why should you make this time commitment to what I've outlined in this book? *Because this program works!* I've seen it work in my own sales work and in the work of the thousands of salespeople who've taken my seminars.

Don't pick and choose. Implement the whole program and see what happens. Don't reinvent the wheel. Ride on it.

Once you've given the program an honest try, write me in care of the publisher, Adams Media, 57 Littlefield Street, Avon, Massachusetts, 02322. Tell me what you think of what I've outlined and how it has worked for you. Either I or someone else in my organization will get back to you.

In the epilogue, you'll find some important observations on moving beyond the close. This section, like the appendices on cold calling, pre-close preparation, and negotiating that follow it, supports the key selling principles we've looked at together in this book. Please read all of this material carefully—then give what I've outlined an honest try!

Beyond the Close

In the first chapter of this book, I began our discussion of closing techniques by noting that finalizing the sale is not a gimmick. I told you that there are—and can be—no "tricks" when it comes to formalizing a business relationship with a prospect or customer. By this point in the book, I hope you understand why I feel so strongly that no salesperson worthy of being called a professional makes the mistake of viewing the entire relationship as one long opportunity to close. I also hope you understand what some of the alternative strategies are.

It's important to remember, too, that there are no "tricks" when it comes to *sustaining* important business relationships over time. This process requires careful thought, insightful analysis, and more than a little creativity. After the business has "closed"—or, to put it more accurately, "opened"—we have to ask ourselves some fundamental questions about the people we're working with.

Sales managers often complain about sales reps who treat friendly (but unqualified) prospects as "sure things." These managers point out, rightly, that it's a mistake to categorize a large percentage of these prospects as likely customers. But there's a similar and less obvious problem salespeople face, one that can be even more serious. How should salespeople categorize the person or organization they're dealing with *after* that person signs on as a customer? We've looked at the four phases of the relationship as it unfolds from our point of view: vendor, supplier, entrenched supplier, partner. But what are the developmental phases the customer goes through?

In most sales organizations, it's too easy for salespeople to ignore any meaningful categorization or analysis of the customers who make commission checks possible. Typically, salespeople assume that, once someone signs on with (or perhaps pays an invoice from) their organization, that person falls into a single, simple category: that of The Customer.

Lots of salespeople speak with pride about the *number* of customers they have. But all too few evaluate the *kinds* of customers they're currently working with.

In my experience, there are three main groups of customers, each with a distinctive outlook, and each requiring a different set of responses from the professional salesperson. (Note: The four categories we discussed in Chapter 16 shed light on *your company's* role in the customer's organization; the three you're about to learn help you understand *your customer's* development over time.)

New Customers

New customers are those who have just agreed to use the product or service. These customers may have made an initial commitment, but they're still evaluating the relationship. If our contact doesn't like what he or she sees, guess what? There's a very good chance we'll be dropped in favor of another supplier. Many new customers still consider themselves in a "trial" period, whether or not we've discussed their business in these terms. In other words, this customer is not really "ours" beyond the initial commitment—unless we can prove that we're worth holding on to.

Not surprisingly, initial experience counts for a great deal with new customers. Even a seemingly trivial customer service or fulfillment problem can have catastrophic effects on these relationships. As salespeople, our objective with members of this group is to get them to feel comfortable working with our organization. We're out to "get them started." To be sure, *all* customers are entitled to consider themselves in the "prove it to me" category, but it's nevertheless true that new customer relationships often stand or fall on the perceptions of the very first interaction with a new supplier. Accordingly, monitoring that first encounter closely, and following up afterwards to discuss overall customer satisfaction, are important parts of any professional salesperson's job. There are often no second chances with this group.

When you're formalizing a relationship with a new customer . . .consider building in a schedule that will demonstrate exactly what's going to happen when . . . and how you will personally monitor the opening phase of the relationship. This provides emotional support and reinforcement. Your aim should be to let the person know that a) you know what service, billing, or follow-through issues are likely to arise, and b) you'll be there to help resolve every potential problem as he or she uses your product or service for the first time. Talk about exactly what's going to happen when the person uses your widget; outline when and how you plan to check in at key points once the person has used what you offer. Then follow through on that plan!

Emerging Customers

Emerging customers are customers with whom we've got an established relationship, but who are only giving us a small portion of the business they could be giving us. Perhaps the customer is a long-term buyer who has simply never moved beyond a certain point. Perhaps something you offered was perceived as delivering less than satisfactory results. Or perhaps this customer started out on a "see what happens" basis, offering us a small piece of the available budget. Or perhaps he or she chose us as a backup supplier. In any event, this customer has been working with us for some time—but hasn't taken any action to move the relationship forward. So, with these customers, our goal is to increase our percentage of the account's total business. Our aim is to learn all we can, build on past successes, and make the case that the *relationship is worth expanding.*

When you're formalizing new business with an emerging customer . . . understand that you probably won't be able to make much progress here until you understand *why* this person is not yet giving you a greater share of the business. There is some reason you're not getting more of this person's budget. Be prepared to step back from "closing"—and ask more questions that will point you toward a fuller understanding of what this customer is currently doing. Is something you currently offer missing the mark with this customer? Can you revise or retarget it? Once you've identified what works, can you highlight appropriate new programs—or expansions of existing programs?

Not long ago we did a training program with a major newspaper. When we followed up with our contacts afterwards, we found that their impression of the program had been that we hadn't customized our message to a particular group of their reps. Rather than simply trying to "close" on another training program with them, we met in person with the key people at the organization. We found out much more about what they wanted to accomplish with that particular group of reps, and designed another program. We delivered it free of charge—and have successfully expanded the relationship since then.

Established Long-Term Customers

Established long-term customers are those with whom we've developed a strong relationship over time and worked successfully to broaden the relationship. There's a greater level of trust in both directions with these customers than with the other two groups. Contacts at these organizations are likely to place a premium on the continuity that working with us offers. Many contacts will also value the knowledge and experience we bring to the table.

The goal here is to maximize those assets in the customer's eyes, solidify our position, and move toward becoming the primary or full supplier. Ideally, we're trying to get to, say, 120 percent of the current business—and, eventually, to become this customer's strategic partner. (Remember the strategic partner stage—the stage where the customer makes us part of the planning process?) To make the most of our relationships with established long-term customers, we must understand, support, and help to fulfill the organization's most important future plans.

When you're formalizing new business with an established long-term customer ... look toward the future. What can you learn that will help you develop a real partnership with your contact and others within the organization? Do all the key people understand how *both* parties stand to benefit by expanding the relationship? At the very least, do you have a good understanding of what you can expect from this account over the next twelve months? Remember, you must have a *deep* understanding of what's going on within the organization to make any partnership work.

So—those are the three main customer groupings. I think you can see from my thumbnail sketches that the three relationships require very different approaches from salespeople and sales managers. Take a look at your list of current customers right now and ask yourself these important questions.

New Customers
- Who is now evaluating (or getting ready to evaluate) a first experience with my organization?
- What can I do to make that first experience a positive one—or at least find out what problems there were?

Emerging Customers
- Who is giving us a relatively small piece of the total business?
- Who else is this customer working with—and why?
- What's my next step to win a larger share?

Established Long-Term Customers
- Who is giving us a significant piece of the total business?
- What's my next step to help this organization fulfill its most important long-term goals?

Some Final Thoughts

"Closing sales" really means building and maintaining relationships. And, truth be told, no relationship worthy of the name could possibly "close" at the very beginning! By the same token, no relationship with a customer (or prospective customer, for that matter) is truly stationary. There's always some new circumstance, some new perspective to explore, some new opportunity.

Earlier in this book, you and I looked at how one-third of all the sales you could conceivably close within a given year *won't* come your way—thanks to events and decisions you really won't have any control over. We compared this state of affairs to that faced by a major-league baseball club, and noted that even a great team—say, the 1927 New York Yankees—managed to lose one-third of its games.

Similarly, one-third of the opportunities for business in a given "season" will wind up going your way. Assuming minimal effort on your part, and barring some spectacular effort to *keep* prospective customers from giving your product or service a try, you're going to work with this one-third. We saw how even a terrible big-league ball club, like the 1962 Mets, somehow managed to win one-third of its games.

The difference between the two teams, we concluded, was that remaining third—the third that top performers manage to win. And here's the thought I want to leave you with as we close the main part of this book:

To win *that* third of the possible business on a regular basis, you must be willing to ask yourself constantly: "What's the next step for my relationship with this prospect or customer?"

If you're talking to someone who's already doing business with you, you must identify whether you're dealing with a new customer, an underachiever, or an established long-term customer, and strategize accordingly, as we've just discussed.

If you're pursuing a brand-new business opportunity, you must accurately determine what stage the emerging relationship really occupies *right now,* and then decide what ought to happen next. Warning: There's no advantage in misleading yourself about what's happening in your contact base. You must be ruthlessly frank about where you stand with each contact!

For instance: Is a "prospect" you spoke with this morning unwilling to commit to any formal next step with you? If the answer is "yes," that person is really an opportunity, a fallback. He or she is someone to call on a month or so down the line to try to set up an appointment, and not an active prospect at all. Eventually, your aim will be to get that person to *become* a prospect. Or suppose you *have* scheduled a first appointment with a new contact. Your aim then becomes to move that person forward to a *second* appointment.

And so it goes. You must develop a reliable "snapshot" of a contact's true status, and then set up a plan for moving forward.

Nothing is static. As long as there are active relationships, there is some opportunity for you to take the initiative, some next course to pursue. Sales is a continual process, a series of mutual advancements that is most efficient when it benefits both parties.

Accepting relentless change means accepting a certain level of uncertainty. Sales is an art, one that's carried out in a continually changing world in which your commitment to advancing the interests of other people is, over time, the defining factor for success.

Winston Churchill once said, "No one can guarantee success in war—one can only deserve it." I believe that, in the final analysis, the same is true of the world of sales. When we accurately identify an opportunity to help another person, and then take active steps to move the relationship closer to the point where we actually *can* help, that's when we begin to deserve success.

Don't worry about extracting verbal "guarantees" from your prospects and customers. Focus instead on finding situations where you honestly believe you can add value, uncovering the most important information, and then committing yourself to doing what must be done to move the relationship forward so you can deliver on that value. If you do that, day in and day out, you will succeed.

Good luck!

Sample Cold Calling Scripts

Initial Contact Script

This is _____; I'm with _____ . I don't know if you've ever heard of us, but we're a nationwide sales training company here in New York City, working with such companies as ABC, DEF, and GHI in the areas of prospect management, cold calling, and selling skills. But the reason I'm calling you specifically, Mr. Prospect, is this: I just finished working with the 123 Bank over in Madison, Wisconsin. And we were very successful in working with their trust department to come up with a way to improve the efficiency of their closing techniques, and frankly what I'd like to do is just stop by next Tuesday and tell you about the ways in which we were successful with that program. How does that sound? Will that work for you? How about 3:00 P.M.?

A Variation on the Preceding Script That Does Not Involve Using as Much Information about Recent Programs

Good morning, _____, this is _____ from _____; we're a sales training firm here in New York City. We've done a lot of work with the ABC, DEF, and GHI companies in the areas of cold calling, prospecting skills, and prospect management. But the reason I'm calling you today is, we just completed work with a number of small manufacturers in Los Angeles; we were able to show them ways in which they could improve their productivity by giving sales training to their sales staffs. What I'd like to do is stop by next Tuesday and tell you about some of the successes we've been having in and around Los Angeles—will this work for you?

Follow-Up Script

Good morning, _____, this is _____ from _____. A number of weeks ago I contacted you, and you asked me to call you back today to set up an appointment. As you may remember, we've been able to do some projects with ABC Company, DEF Associates, and GHI Group, and we've been able to show some really remarkable results in increasing their sales figures. Would Tuesday at 3:00 P.M. be good for you?

Referral Script

Good morning, _____, this is _____ from _____. Let me tell you why I'm calling you. The other day I was meeting with _____ at _____ and we were discussing a number of projects we had just completed for _____. He said that I should really contact you as you are absolutely the right person to talk to about projects in this area. Can we get together? How about Tuesday at 3:00 P.M.?

Sample Sales Dialogues

Here is a complete sales scenario, complete with the requisite small talk and resistance from the prospect. Don't think of this as a "script." The problem with "selling scripts" is that prospects and customers usually don't know their lines! Think of what follows as a model for developing a good conversation. That's what makes closing possible.

First Appointment

You: Hello, how are you?

Prospect: Fine.

You: Good to meet you.

Prospect: Nice to meet you, too.

You: I had an interesting time getting over here because of the traffic; do you guys have a lot of traffic around here?

Prospect: Always—they are doing major construction this year on Main Street. There is a lot of traffic.

You: Really? Now, do you live far from here?

Prospect: I live about an hour away, and these days it's about an hour and a half with the traffic—it's really trouble. Do you want to sit down?

You: Thanks. I walked through the building—you have an interesting facility. What do you actually do? You manufacture chairs?

Prospect: Yes, we manufacture chairs and office furniture. We design and produce all kinds of furniture: everything for an office top to bottom, and for upper-scale organizations and executive offices, too.

You: No kidding. How long have you been in the business?

Prospect: We've been in business for twenty-five years.

You: Really?

Prospect: And we've grown from a mom-and-pop business at the beginning to the point now where we are to bring the company public in a few months.

You: No kidding, that's fantastic. Okay. Do you remember our telephone conversation at all?

Prospect: Not really.

You: Let me ask you a question. Would it help if I tell you something about me and my company first?

Prospect: Yeah, that would definitely be helpful.

You: Let me give you a little background. We've been in business for the last twenty-two years, and we've worked with about a thousand different companies selling our widgets. One of the things we've found is that our widgets have been extremely beneficial in a number of areas. I'm just curious though, in the past have you ever bought widgets from an outside vendor?

Prospect: We tend to do everything on the inside whenever we can.

You: That's unusual. Why is that?

Prospect: To save money; we believe that it saves us money.

You: Uh huh.

Prospect: And it's just one of those things; that's just the way we've done it for years.

You: No kidding, and you still manufacture X, Y, and Z? How many widgets are you using today?

Prospect: Hmm, I have to think.

You: The reason I'm asking is, I've been working with a number of companies, and, you know, it's something that they found needed to be revisited based upon current demand.

Prospect: We've been really backed up—we have a lot of orders for some reason for the upcoming year. We've been so bombarded that we haven't taken the time to analyze it. We've increased from our normal widget use, which is about twenty-five a day, and we've gone up to seventy-five to 100.

You: Have you really?

Prospect: Yeah, but we just haven't had time to think about it.

You: That's incredible. That seems like a lot of work.

Prospect: Yeah, it has been. We just got the report last week when we realized that we had to place more material orders.

You: You know, when I was driving up, I realized there seem to be more trucks around your building than there were a year ago. It seems to me that you're growing.

Prospect: Yes, like I mentioned, this year has been crazy. We haven't had a chance to sit down. We're going public and we're growing. It's just hectic.

You: I'm just curious how, you know—you look like you actually like this kind of job. I mean, it seems like an exciting company. How did you get this job? Why do you stay here?

Prospect: Well, first of all I love the business. Actually, my grandfather started the business and left it ten years ago.

You: Really.

Prospect: Then, it went out of the family. Other people were managing it and running it, and then I came back into it after I got my MBA. I just love this company so much.

You: How long have you been back?

Prospect: I've been back for six years.

You: Is it working out the way you expected it to?

Prospect: Better; this going public thing is my baby, and I'm enjoying it.

You: And the decision to produce your own widgets—that really came from some years back?

Prospect: Yeah. It's been like that for many years, and like I said before, we've never had the time to think about it, it has always been so hectic.

You: You never thought about doing that outside?

Prospect: No. The fact is, you know, when you called, that's probably why I made the appointment; it was probably a thought to go outside.

You: I'll tell you what my thinking is and the reason why I'm asking you all this. We have been working with other manufacturers, and what we are finding is that the widgets we produce really have been able to save them time and money. But more importantly, they actually enhance the overall productivity and the value of the end product being sold.

But let me go back to one thing: In the past you typically manufactured from here, but if you would change, would that drastically impact the people who are working here? I don't want to do something to throw somebody off.

Prospect: Well, it could, it could. There are three people who are involved in taking the material, and creating the widget which then goes into the rest of the machinery. But the truth is, I wanted to promote them and get other people to do this, because it is kind of grunt work.

You: Having worked with a lot of manufacturers before, I think that there are a host of things that we can produce for you to help you.

Prospect: Well, yes. But can I tell you something really honestly? The only hesitation I have, even with just talking to you, is the quality. We know when we make it inside that we are not going to have any problems in that area, and of course we never did it on the outside. Other companies in the industry have had problems, as you know, with their widgets, so quality is an issue. Actually, doing it inside wasn't really that big a deal.

You: Would you mind if I showed you one of our widgets? Let me just show you this—take a look at this. I think the thing that I like best when you look at widgets, one of things that this widget does, which probably no other widget does, is that it has this little hinge here. See that? That's patented. That's an input-output control flow through valve. That's what keeps our quality standard the highest in the industry.

Now, if I were thinking about making widgets for you, I would try to make a widget that featured that hinge.

Prospect: The only thing is, when I look at that picture, I don't know what size that is, but we tend to need it larger.

You: Uh huh . . . larger . . .

Prospect: Because of our machines. I'll tell you our situation. We have some rebuilds, which are the old machine version, and we have some new machines. That's why we need primarily larger widgets than the size you have. And I think some might have to be customized.

You: How much larger are you talking about?

Prospect: Probably three to six inches bigger than that.

You: Take a look at this—if we did it this way would that work?

Prospect: How about a little smaller?

You: A little smaller, okay . . . Say, I'll tell you what. Let's change the configurations, and come back with a 350 over 90, like this model. And if we did this configuration I think this would do what you wanted.

Prospect: Right. Because then I could use it for the older machinery *and* the newer machinery.

You: You know what? It might help. Let me tell you something. I think it might help if you and I went into the plant now; that way I could see how this whole thing operates, and what it looks like, and how your people are actually using what we're talking about.

Prospect: Yeah, if you are going to customize it, I would love for you to come with me now, and really look at everything and make sure it's right.

You: Okay, let's do that.

• • •

You: It was really interesting what you showed me, what I found out about how you actually do business.

Prospect: Oh, yeah. I mean people think that we're this little specialty place, but when you go down on the floor it's just another world.

You: Yeah, it really is interesting what you do. I have an idea, and you tell me how you think this works. I could come back with a proposal, because I think that you could use about 500 of the widgets at any given time. What I would like to do is come back some time in the next ten days, probably next week, if that's all right with you.

Prospect: Wait, let me check my calendar.

You: But let me tell you what I'll do. Let me come back and bring you not a proposal but an outline. What I like to do is sit down with Jill, Andy and maybe I'll get

Steve involved in this, and actually develop an outline of how I think this would work. That way we'll be one step before the proposal still.

Prospect: I'll get my production manager in on this.

You: Would you?

Prospect: Yeah.

You: Why don't we do this. Let's get together next Thursday. Let me come back with an outline. Let me also put together some prices.

Prospect: Okay, that would be very helpful.

You: By the way, just out of curiosity, typically when you look at your pricing structure now, how would you say it's running?

Prospect: It's been between ten and twenty per gross, depending on quantity.

You: Is it really? Okay, let me play with that. Okay, let me come back, let me work from this, and let's talk next week, if you don't mind. I might call you beforehand just to run a couple things by you.

Prospect: Oh, yeah, that will be fine.

You: Okay, let's get together Thursday, let me show you what my thinking is, and we'll see if we can go from there.

Prospect: Okay, that sounds great . . . Can we make it for 11:00 on Thursday?

You: That would be great. And what I might do is bring Lynne with me. I'm not sure, but we'll talk about that later.

Prospect: Okay, does Lynne know this stuff?

You: Lynne is great. I'll tell you one of the reasons why I'm asking that. Lynne has had experience in this area before and she might have a different take on this. . . but in any case, I'll review this with her. Let's play it out and let me come next week and we'll go from there.

Prospect: Okay.

You: Great, thanks a lot.
Prospect: Thank you.

Second Appointment

You: Good to see you again.
Prospect: Hi.
You: How are you?
Prospect: Our production manager couldn't join us—we had a little incident on the floor.
You: Uh oh.
Prospect: But he really did give me some information, and we discussed the issues, and now we are really eager to see what you have come up with.
You: All right. Okay, let me tell you what I did, let me tell you what happened. I went back to the office and met with Steve, Lynne, and Jill.
Prospect: Was Lynne going to meet with us?
You: She had to take a rain check. Next time, maybe she will be able to get together with us. In any case, what happened was, I talked to her and what we came up with was this. I didn't do a proposal, what I did was a preproposal, an outline, as we discussed, and basically what I did was structure. I set out on what I thought your objective was, how I thought we might work together, what I thought the cost would be, what I think the savings might be to you ultimately, and a shot at a production schedule. That's how I put this together. And I would like to run this by you and if you like it we can go ahead.

Okay, anyway, let me go through this with you if that's okay. Here's my copy, here's yours. All right, now, let me show you how it happens. Based on the problem that we talked about, first of all, this is what I think our objectives are, what I think you want to do, at least what I understand about your objective, but it's possible you might want to change it.

Prospect: Right.

You: Okay, so you agree with what we have laid out here?

Prospect: Yeah. I think you've hit it on the head.

You: Now, the second thing was to analyze the situation. We went in there, we looked at it, we talked and we looked at the model TJ38 as a possibility. We felt that this was the kind of program that would work for you. So, this is what it is. So, I figure that now what we want to suggest is the program where you are using us on a level here, which will produce this kind of result. And that's a range I think would make sense.

Prospect: Um, not really. I mean it does but it doesn't.

You: Tell me what you think.

Prospect: Well, in terms of quantity on the initial shipment.

You: Uh huh.

Prospect: You know, you base that directly on what we are using now, and we're going public; we have a small storage area.

You: Uh huh.

Prospect: We could increase that at the end. But at first that might be kind of high.

You: Okay.

Prospect: Yeah.

You: Okay, let's cross this off. Now I'm a little worried about this part. Do you like this element here, element three, that says the minimum will be 14,000?

Prospect: Yes, that I liked.

You: Okay, but this you don't like.

Prospect: No . . . just because it wouldn't be enough, I need a good sampling to start it, not large quantities.

You: Okay, what about item number four, does that make sense to you?

Prospect: Um, not really, no.

You: No . . . Okay, let's take that out, let's take out items four and five.

Prospect: Uh huh.

You: Here's a plan we've used with some of our customers. Take a look at this. (Pause.) Now this is what I would say. I would rather see you do it this way. What do you think about that?

Prospect: Ah, that's better.

You: Do you think that makes sense?

Prospect: Uh huh.

You: Let's get rid of three and four, and let me add this item.

Prospect: Uh huh.

You: Does that make sense?

Prospect: Yeah, now that little thing . . . is that the test drum?

You: Yes.

Prospect: Could we do that . . . How soon could you do that if I'd agree?

You: Well, I could speed up the process, I had thought about this timetable over here, and here was my conclusion at the time. I thought this would work okay. I thought that Tom could do about ninety and if you want to, he could do about eighty . . . even sixty if you wanted that.

Prospect: I think eighty would be fine.

You: Okay, that works with an eighty-day max. Now that we move down to here, here's the cost . . . my estimation is it will cost you about this much. So that's how I see the cost coming out. Here's my point—and I will show you the other piece of this outline—my point is, based on this cost, this will save you about three cents per unit, which you will multiply by 150,000. You start to see what happens. That's why my question on this part over here . . . now at first I wasn't happy with that number.

Prospect: Yeah, that is a bit high.

You: Okay, I wasn't happy with that. I thought we could do better. When I went back to John, he thought if you commit to this minimum purchase, I could change that number which would reduce the cost to about here.

Prospect: Let me ask you something.

You: Yeah.

Prospect: Um . . . once we go public in a few months, we'll have the cash.

You: Right.

Prospect: But right now that's a lot of money for us . . . doing it ourselves, you know, the cost is kind of spread out.

You: Right. Uh huh.

Prospect: Could we do that for the test? Do the test run for the lower, at the lower price, and make up for it later?

You: That's an issue. Suppose I billed it out, not immediately, suppose I give you sixty days on the billing process. Zero up front, you stay with this piece that we talked about, but I give you sixty days without any kind of payment and then, assuming everything is all right, we will drop the whole payment in at that point. Is that better for your cash flow?

Prospect: Yeah, actually that would work out very well.

You: All right.

Prospect: We can get the bank's signature, if you need to.

You: Now, I know your brother is involved in production, did you talk to him at all about this?

Prospect: Yeah, Bill wanted to see the pricing.

You: That would be no problem.

Prospect: And make sure it's in his budget. He said it would probably get rid of the grunt work.

You: Yeah, okay. Let me ask you a question, should we go to Bill?

Prospect: No, it's not necessary.

You: If I come back with a proposal and I write this up, will Bill have any problems, or do you think that's a concern?

Prospect: Um, I don't think so. Bill is very . . . Since I've come on he has always helped me with anything. When I brought this up, he said "Great" . . . and to be honest with you, actually, I would make that decision. As it turns out, my brother is not going to be involved in this company much longer.

You: Really.

Prospect: He wants to go outside and do some consulting on his own. We believe it will work out for the best for everyone.

You: Okay. So let's do this. Let me take what we have just done now and, if you agree with this, we will look at these basic components. Let me put this together in a full proposal, let me come back in . . . give me a week or so, because I have to get it all set up on the computer.

Prospect: Okay.

You: And then what I want to do is begin to think about how we would put this together. I'll tell you what I'm going to do, if you don't mind. I would like to start to reserve this inventory. Now I know you don't need it for another ninety days, so what I'd like to do is hold that initial quantity in abeyance, so we have it. That way it's not a problem meeting your schedule.

Prospect: Um, I'm not so sure about that.

You: Why? Tell me.

Prospect: Just because I have to see the proposal, see everything before I just commit to that.

You: Well, okay.

Prospect: With the real pricing.

You: Okay, so the cost might be a concern. Let's go back to this. If that's a concern then what . . . I guess what I'm asking you is, what would make this work better?

Prospect: Well, you analyzed the cost.

You: Right.

Prospect: On how much we would save, and the savings aren't that great.

You: Okay.

Prospect: It's good, but it's not a lot. I have gotten some literature from your competitors and . . .

You: Have you talked to the Johnsons?

Prospect: I didn't talk to them, I talked to the Petersons.

You: Oh really. Oh.

Prospect: They didn't send a salesperson or anything like that, but they did send me literature.

You: I have to tell you something—they have very good prices. I can't argue with that.

Prospect: And I have to consider that. And quality, too, of course.

You: Okay.

Prospect: What I would love to do is speak to some of your customers.

You: I'll tell you what I would do. I have my references here, let me give you the list. Call them, I think you'll like what you hear. I have to be honest—I see this as making a lot of sense for your organization.

Prospect: Uh huh. Um, well, maybe I just really want to see the proposal.

You: Okay. That's fair.

Prospect: That would make me feel better.

You: Okay, then let's get together.

Prospect: Okay.

You: Okay, let's do this, do you have your calendar? Let's get together the eighth.

Prospect: Okay.

You: Let me come back, let me put a whole proposal together. I am still going to block out this inventory at our risk and I will tell you why: because if I make you want to say you want to do this, I would like to have the inventory for you.

Prospect: Okay, that's fair. I don't want to make you go out on a limb, though . . .

You: No, no. I just wanted to make sure you're okay if it goes through, that's all. And that's our risk.

Prospect: Okay.

You: Okay. I'll see you on the eighth. Let me bring back the proposal and we'll discuss it. Look, if you think Bill should be here, we can always have him come in, if that's not a hassle, but we'll work that out.

Prospect: Yeah. Bill could drop by.

You: Okay, good. See you next week.

Prospect: Okay.

You: Thanks a lot.

Third Appointment

You: How are you?

Prospect: Good.

You: That's great. I gotta tell you something. I was very happy with our last meeting. I thought it went well and I like everything that we did.

Prospect: Yeah. I mean the truth is that I've never been with a salesperson who showed me such detailed attention and came back again.

You: I appreciate that.

Prospect: They mostly come in and give pricing and leave. That's it.

You: You know what's helpful. It's helpful for me to understand what you do, and the way you do it, and how you do it, and where you do it, and who you do it with. So finding out about all that really gave me some information. Let me tell you what I have in my briefcase. In my briefcase I have a proposal for you that I think is right. I went ahead and I changed a couple of the minor things I talked about that I wanted to make right, and basically I think you're going to like what I have. I feel very comfortable with it.

Prospect: Good.

You: Let me show you. Here it is. On the first page is a letter saying we want to do business with you. I just want you to know that whatever else we do, I would love to do business with you. This simply says what we pretty much outlined. Here is a little about us, who we are, what we do. Okay, here is the product we've designed for you, TJ38 minus 3, and here we're saying here is the quantity. This is what it's going to look like.

Prospect: Do you have that sixty-day thing?

You: Yes, that's right here.

Prospect: Yeah, okay. Let's get started.

You: Thank you very much.

Prospect: Okay. Thank you.

Seven Questions You Should Be Able to Answer about Your Prospect Before You Try to Close the Deal

Why do salespeople fall into the trap of attempting to close the sale with silly "closing tricks"—like saying "I'll lose my job if you don't buy from me?" The short answer is that they're afraid. Specifically, they're afraid the prospect will turn them down if they ask for the business straightforwardly. So to overcome this fear, they practice delivering some manipulative, supposedly foolproof "technique" that somehow will magically make the person say "Yes."

The truth is, their fear about asking for the business is usually well justified. Most salespeople who try to close the deal don't yet *know enough* about the other person to ask for the business.

Here are seven questions you should be sure to ask your prospect before you attempt to close any sale. If you don't know the answers, you're not yet ready to make a formal recommendation. You should get face-to-face with your prospect, pull out your pen and your yellow legal pad, and *find out* the answers.

And by the way . . . asking these questions also serves an important purpose during the course of your discussion with the prospect. By posing a question that addresses one of the following issues and then taking notes on the response you receive, you regain control of the conversation and put yourself in a better position to make a recommendation about the next step in the relationship.

1. *How did this person get this job?*

Was your contact one of the founders of the company? Was he or she recruited by a pricey executive search firm? Did he or she answer a classified ad a month and a half ago? Your aim here is to determine your contact's level of influence.

2. *What's the person's role in the organization?*

Is your contact a leader or a follower? What part did he or she play in the past when it came to deciding whether and how to use companies like yours? What major projects is he or she working on right now? If the person you're talking to does not have any projects that are relevant to your selling area, you are not talking to the right person. Your aim here is to find out what this person can or cannot do within the organization.

3. *Are you dealing with someone who is either a) a decision maker or b) a person who can get the decision made for you?*

If your contact has no knowledge, access, or influence relating to your product or service, you need to find a way to get this person to help you connect with someone else in the organization. Your aim here is to identify who, in the organization, is likely to be able to help you get this deal done—and to determine with some certainty whether your contact falls into that category.

4. *What's the organization's current plan for dealing with the area where you hope to make a contribution?*

To find out, ask, "What were you planning to do this quarter in order to . . .?" Your aim here is to identify any competitors who may already be involved, and to get a sense of how the target organization has defined the problem up to this point.

5. *Why aren't they using you already?*

Your aim here is twofold: to learn what the company already knows or thinks about your organization, and to find out what plans are already in place. (To this extent, there is a certain amount of overlap between this question and #4.) I suggest that, early on in the relationship, you ask some variation on this question: "I checked my records and I noticed you're not using us right now. I'm just curious—why not?" While you're at it, you could also find out if the company ever *considered* working with you or getting in touch with you in the past. You may have been on the short list for a project and not even known about it.

6. *Does this deal truly make sense to the other person?*

The goal here is to find out whether you're on your own or whether you've got an ally. Sometimes salespeople ask, "How am I supposed to know whether or not what I'm proposing makes sense to the other person?" The answer is actually very simple. When the prospect begins to act as though closing the sale is as important to him or her as it is to you . . . you'll know it makes sense! I like to find out whether what I'm discussing with a prospect really makes sense by asking a question like this as I'm on the way out the door after a second meeting: "Listen, just between you and me, how do you think this is going to turn out?"

7. *What does your contact think is going to happen next?*
The main idea here is to get very clear on what the mutually agreed-upon next step in the relationship is. If your contact has no idea you're about to close the deal, there's a problem. Here's a good selling rule: *Never make a presentation you don't think will close!* Try saying something like this: "You know, based on what we've gone over today, I have to say that this really makes sense to me. I'm thinking that the next time we get together, on Tuesday at 2:00, we'll go over all the changes and I'll show you our full proposal, and at that point, *I* think it's going to make sense for us to reserve the training dates. What do *you* think?"

Six Tactical Questions You Should Be Able to Answer about Any Prospect You Plan to Close

Here are six questions you should be able to answer from your side of the closing equation. Answering these questions will help you to establish the right *plan* for closing the deal. If you don't have detailed answers to one or more of these questions, it means that you haven't developed a strong enough strategy to be able to make a formal recommendation yet.

1. *What are the most relevant success stories for this particular organization?*

You should, of course, have a number of success stories in your "arsenal." For instance, you should know exactly why your organization's #1 customer decided to buy from you, and you should be ready to discuss that account in detail.

But these basic success stories aren't always the most relevant from the prospect's point of view. Do a little digging and find out which of your company's current clients or customers offers the closest match with your current prospect. Then be ready to talk about that customer in depth.

2. *What do I know for certain about past buying patterns/decisions at this organization?*

If your meetings and discussions haven't told you anything meaningful about the *how* of this organization's buying process, you have more homework to do. How, specifically, will the decision maker(s) at this organization be evaluating you? What yardsticks will they be using? Have they been talking to anyone else? If so, how did they choose that organization to talk to?

3. *What do I want to happen next?*

You must have a clear Next Step in mind—something you want the prospect or the target organization to do. If that doesn't work out, you should be able to suggest a good backup Next Step. Will you conclude the next meeting by asking for . . .

- A meeting to review a preliminary proposal with the prospect?
- A meeting to introduce the prospect to your boss (or a technical expert within your organization)?
- A meeting to demonstrate your product or service?
- A commitment from the prospect to visit your facility or attend one of your company's events?

Choose your proposed Next Step carefully, and match it to what you've learned about the prospect. Often, when we can't secure a Next Step, it's because we ask for one that's TOO DIFFICULT or NOT HELPFUL ENOUGH to the contact.

4. *If I'm presenting before a committee, which attendees can I talk to or learn more about before the meeting, and how should I follow through afterwards?*

Ask your primary contact for guidance and help in dealing with committees. *Before the meeting takes place,* you should try to schedule a follow-through meeting to discuss the meeting and evaluate how it went with your primary contact. ("I'm really looking forward to the meeting on Wednesday. Why don't you and I schedule a half hour right now to get together on Friday so we can evaluate where things stand. Could we meet on Friday at 2:00?")

5. *What questions/issues should I anticipate? How will I turn them around?*

Review the prospects and customers who are most similar to the organization you will be meeting with. Ask yourself: What obstacles came up that time? What questions did I have to resolve? What difficulties is my contact likely to have in "selling" this to his or her constituency?

Based on what worked best for previous customers and prospects, see if you can develop a plan for helping this prospect to deal with each of the potential challenges you uncover.

6. *What will my opening be?*

Know how you plan to open the meeting! Then . . . practice your opening!

Your best bet is to offer an overview of how you plan to address critical goals that the prospect has identified for you: "We've put together a proposal that is designed to help your team hit or exceed their quota for this year. We plan to use three customized training programs to do that: Appointment Making, Getting to 'Closed,' and High Efficiency Selling Skills. Today, I plan to show you how each of those programs would be delivered."

Eight Foundation Principles of Effective Negotiating

1. The goal of negotiating is to end up with a better deal than could have been achieved without negotiating.
2. An effective daily prospecting routine improves your negotiating position.
3. To negotiate effectively, you must be able to identify the most important interests of each side.
4. To negotiate effectively, you must be able to develop creative options that allow both sides to broadcast a "win" to their constituents (boss, colleagues, shareholders, etc).
5. To negotiate effectively, you must be able to identify an outcome that both sides will recognize as "fair."
6. "Knee-jerk" discounting of price is the lowest form of negotiation.
7. You must never enter a potential negotiating meeting without a backup plan.
8. The next best thing to actually negotiating from a position of strength is acting as though you are negotiating from a position of strength.

Eleven Practical Ru ~~~~ Negotiating the Best Deal

Rule #1: Know when you're willing to walk away.

How strong is your negotiating position? You can really only negotiate from a position of strength if you really could walk away . . . *and* the prospect/client would prefer that you didn't. For every negotiating discussion, try to identify your best alternative to a negotiated agreement.

Rule #2: Know when to delay.

The bigger the deal, the more delay there needs to be between the original offer and the negotiated offer. On important deals, consider letting twenty-four hours elapse between offer and counteroffer.

Rule #3: Avoid negotiating against yourself.

Negotiating against yourself is what happens when you're negotiating in good faith, but the other side feels it doesn't have to—and you keep making concessions in order to keep the discussions going.

Rule #4: Be prepared to name and defend your price.

As salespeople, we must be ready to make the first move and name our opening price, rather than expecting the potential buyer to outline his or her budget for us. We must also be prepared to explain our price structure, so that it is not ceived as an arbitrary figure. We must be prepared to answer these questions: What are the elements that go into our pricing? Why is it a fair price?

Rule #5: Never offer to discount.

It's easy to discount—but it's a poor negotiating strategy to offer a price concession that no one has asked for. If your negotiation efforts are not built around interests like long-term profitability or sustained market success—or if your low price does not gain you access to future high-volume deals—consider walking away from the negotiations.

Rule #6: Negotiate terms before you negotiate price.

Offer to change payment terms before you agree to reduce your price. Think of the last time a customer demanded and got a price concession from you. How could you have developed a counteroffer involving payment terms before agreeing to the discount?

Rule #7: Don't give up something for nothing.

Even a small concession should result in a parallel concession from the other side. Think of a time when you "threw in" a concession without getting anything in return for it. How else could you have moved the discussions forward?

Rule #8: Don't get hung up on ROI.

Don't waste too much time and energy trying to show exactly how your product or service will pay for itself in X months. Instead, focus on the measurable benefits of what you offer and how your organization will support the buying organization over time, as part of a long-term partnership.

Rule #9: Help the individual look good.

Consider not only the organizational interests, but also the personal interests of your negotiating partner. What is this person's relationship to his or her boss, staff, or other constituents? What does he or she wish to change in terms of power, status, personal goals, or career goals? Is he or she out to prove something to someone? If so, what?

Rule #10: Never change the price without changing the deal.

When pressured to reduce your price, do so only after making some kind of alteration in your plan. Ask yourself: If I must change the price, how, specifically, would I reorganize the deal? And what is the lowest dollar figure I would accept before walking away?

Rule #11: Before you start negotiating, practice reconfiguring your product/service options.

How many different ways could you bundle an offering to a current prospect? You should be prepared, at any given moment, to prepare at least five different configurations you could present to a current prospect.

This is an extremely important skill. You should practice reconfiguring your product and service packages for two simple reasons: first, to defend your pricing, and second, to protect yourself against an apples-to-apples comparison with your competition. Be ready, willing, and able to use your company's resources to develop "alternate" or "backup" plans.

The Sales Negotiation Model

Moving from an initial proposal to a final agreement should take the path shown in the diagram on page 143. Principles to follow include:

- At each level, you should only give up something in exchange for something else.
- Every new proposal or suggestion from you must be based on their response to what has come before.
- Every negative response from them should be replied to with the question, "What *will* work?"
- If deadlocked, consider pulling back and setting another date/time to resume negotiation.

Also keep in mind the following facts about what you do and don't know about the two sides in a negotiation.

What We Know about Our Situation

1. What our ideal outcome for the agreement looks like.
2. At what point we'd walk away.
3. How we can bundle our products/services differently, and what no-cost resources we can add.

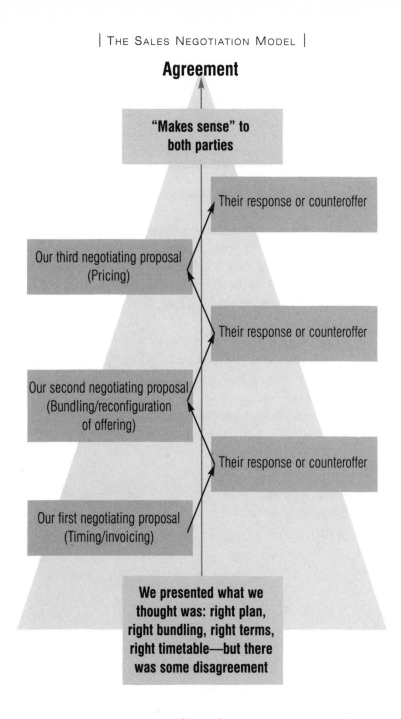

The Sales Negotiation Model

Agreement

"Makes sense" to both parties

Their response or counteroffer

Our third negotiating proposal (Pricing)

Their response or counteroffer

Our second negotiating proposal (Bundling/reconfiguration of offering)

Their response or counteroffer

Our first negotiating proposal (Timing/invoicing)

We presented what we thought was: right plan, right bundling, right terms, right timetable—but there was some disagreement

4. Our company's top-line, bottom-line, and market share goals.
5. What we've presented to this person or group.
6. That our price *does* work for other customers in this market.

What We Know about Their Situation

1. The other side has a negotiating goal, but we don't know what it is. (Possibilities include: Wrap up the deal quickly, impress the boss, achieve X result with Y available dollars.) There may be individual negotiating goals and organizational negotiating goals operating at the same time.
2. The other side has a walkaway point—but we don't know what it is. (Possibilities include: Spend absolutely no more than $25,000 in budget; program must begin by April 1, etc.)
3. Whether they've bought from us in the past.

Index

About the Author

STEPHAN SCHIFFMAN has trained more than 350,000 salespeople at firms such as AT&T Information Systems, Chemical Bank, Manufacturers Hanover Trust, Motorola, and U.S. Healthcare. Mr. Schiffman, president of D.E.I. Management Group, is the author of *Cold Calling Techniques (That Really Work!)*, *The 25 Sales Habits of Highly Successful Salespeople*, and several other popular books on sales.

Do you have questions, comments, or suggestions regarding this book? Please share them with me! Write to me at this address:

Stephan Schiffman
c/o Adams Media
57 Littlefield Street
Avon, MA 02322

Cold Calling Techniques (That Really Work!), Fifth Edition

In today's changing marketplace, smart salespeople know that cold calling is more than just picking up the phone—and great salespeople know that the secret to success is technique. The fifth edition of *Cold Calling Techniques* reveals tried and true methods for reaching high-level executives and making the sale. Sales guru Stephan Schiffman provides readers with field-tested strategies for sure-fire cold calling tactics that increase sales, including:

- Creating a comfortable, workable system
- Honing phone prospecting techniques
- Reaching the decision-makers
- Getting the appointment
- Making a winning pitch
- Perfecting the "follow-through"
- Increasing call volume
- Improving the closing ratio
- Beating the competition

Featuring updated information about the newest technology trends, *Cold Calling Techniques* offers simple, effective solutions to a challenge all sales representatives face.

ISBN: 1-58062-856-7, Trade paperback, $9.95 ($15.95 CAN)

The Consultant's Handbook, Second Edition

*T*he *Consultant's Handbook* is the
definitive resource for those who
want to enter one of today's most
exciting, challenging, and potentially
lucrative fields—consulting.

- Should you or shouldn't you incorporate?
- What are the advantages of working with a partner?
- Should you advertise?
- What are the best and least expensive ways to attract clients?

For most people, not knowing the correct
answers to these questions—and dozens more like them—can lead to
expensive mistakes. Hit or miss reactions to critical business problems cost
beginning consultants money, clients, time, and in far too many cases, their
practices. *The Consultant's Handbook* provides an authoritative, balanced
appraisal of the benefits as well as the pitfalls you can expect to encounter
in this dynamic field.

Stephan Schiffman, himself a highly successful consultant, shows you how to:

- Predict and prepare for the most common business problems you're likely to face
- Attract clients during the first crucial months of your practice with virtually no marketing budget.
- Determine what rates you should charge—and how you should collect your fees
- Write winning proposals that encourage repeat business
- Identify your market base, and avoid scattershot marketing campaigns

ISBN: 1-58062-441-3, Trade paperback, $12.95 ($18.95 CAN)

The 25 Sales Habits of Highly Successful Salespeople, 2nd Edition

This title demonstrates how most successful salespeople practice powerful, effective sales techniques—and shows you how to make these techniques part of your own set of selling skills. From tips on developing selling plans to strategies for getting quality referrals, Schiffman's advice can help you sell more. Stephan Schiffman's techniques are practical, relevant, and easy to apply.

ISBN: 1-55850-391-9, Trade paperback, $6.95 ($9.95 CAN)

The 25 Most Common Sales Mistakes (and How to Avoid Them), 2nd Edition

Are you losing sales you should have made? Most salespeople are! Why? They make fundamental mistakes—ranging from failing to really listen to potential clients to failing to stay in touch after a sale. Stephan Schiffman's clear, concise, easy-to-use handbook shows you how to identify and correct these costly errors.

ISBN: 1-55850-511-3, Trade paperback, $6.95 ($9.95 CAN)

The 25 Most Dangerous Sales Myths (and How to Avoid Them)

In his latest addition to the highly successful 25 Sales Skills series, America's #1 corporate sales trainer debunks the 25 most popular myths that cost salespeople money every day. By avoiding these myths and knowing the truth behind them, salespeople will improve their pitch and strengthen their sales calls.

ISBN: 1-59337-014-8, Trade paperback, $6.95 ($10.95 CAN)

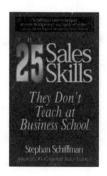

Power Sales Presentations

A step-by-step guide to preparing and delivering powerful sales presentations. Includes examples of real-life dialogues that show you just what not to say, and how to respond to a prospect's questions or comments. *Power Sales Presentations* provides an overview of the entire in-person selling process for sales professionals in all industries. It is the perfect companion to the author's more specialized books on cold calling and telemarketing.

ISBN: 1-55850-252-1, Trade paperback, $7.95 ($11.95 CAN)

Stephan Schiffman's Telesales, 2nd Edition

Stephan Schiffman is back with an improved, updated edition for the new millennium! From getting started, to the five ways to increase income, to defining a prospect, to closing a sale, the guru of sales teaches how to transform the telesales process. This complete reference shows how to identify the true definition of selling, determine a strict—but workable—set of criteria for tracking active prospects, implement a powerful new communication strategy to turn around initial negative responses, and much more!

ISBN: 1-58062-813-3, Trade paperback, $10.95 ($17.95 CAN)